T0318958

Cambridge Elements ☰

Elements in Politics and Society in Southeast Asia
edited by
Edward Aspinall
Australian National University
Meredith L. Weiss
University at Albany, SUNY

MEDIA AND POWER IN SOUTHEAST ASIA

Cherian George
Hong Kong Baptist University
Gayathry Venkiteswaran
University of Nottingham, Malaysia Campus

CAMBRIDGE
UNIVERSITY PRESS

CAMBRIDGE
UNIVERSITY PRESS

University Printing House, Cambridge CB2 8BS, United Kingdom

One Liberty Plaza, 20th Floor, New York, NY 10006, USA

477 Williamstown Road, Port Melbourne, VIC 3207, Australia

314–321, 3rd Floor, Plot 3, Splendor Forum, Jasola District Centre, New Delhi – 110025, India

79 Anson Road, #06–04/06, Singapore 079906

Cambridge University Press is part of the University of Cambridge.

It furthers the University's mission by disseminating knowledge in the pursuit of education, learning, and research at the highest international levels of excellence.

www.cambridge.org
Information on this title: www.cambridge.org/9781108467889
DOI: 10.1017/9781108665643

First published 2019

A catalogue record for this publication is available from the British Library.

ISBN 978-1-108-46788-9 Paperback
ISSN 2515-2998 (online)
ISSN 2515-298X (print)

Media and Power in Southeast Asia

Elements in Politics and Society in Southeast Asia

DOI: 10.1017/9781108665643
First published online: August 2019

Cherian George
Hong Kong Baptist University

Gayathry Venkiteswaran
University of Nottingham Malaysia

Author for correspondence: Cherian George, cherian@cantab.net

Abstract: This study of Southeast Asian media and politics explores issues of global relevance pertaining to journalism's relationship with political power. It argues that the development of free, independent, and plural media has been complicated by trends towards commercialisation, digital platforms, and identity-based politics. These forces interact with state power in complex ways, opening up political space and pluralising discourse, but without necessarily producing structural change. The Element has sections on the democratic transitions of Indonesia, Myanmar and Malaysia; authoritarian resilience in Singapore; media ownership patterns in non-communist Southeast Asia; intolerance in Indonesia and Myanmar; and digital disruptions in Vietnam and Malaysia.

Keywords: news media, journalism, political communication, politics, Internet

ISBNs: 9781108467889 (PB), 9781108665643 (OC)
ISSNs: 2515-2998 (online), 2515-298X (print)

Contents

1 Southeast Asia's Contested Media Space   1

2 Media and Democratic Transitions   10

3 Authoritarian Resilience and Media   21

4 Big Business and Media   31

5 Media and Intolerance   41

6 Digital Media Disruptions   52

Bibliography   63

1 Southeast Asia's Contested Media Space

Any study of media systems will inevitably be coloured by the perceptions and preoccupations of the time. Media do not stand apart from politics, economics, culture, and society. As these change, so too do our expectations and estimations of media. If we were writing in the 1970s, we would probably be focusing on the media's role in the grand enterprises of nation-building and economic development that then defined the zeitgeist of postcolonial Asia. We would be assessing how the region's newspapers and broadcasters were faring against the economic and cultural imperialism of Western powers, and probably using the concept of 'development journalism' to analyse the media's contribution to largely state-driven socio-economic progress. If, on the other hand, this were the 1990s, the inescapable backdrop would be the democratic wave sweeping the globe following the end of the Cold War. Intellectual fashion would have dictated that we relate our study to the notion of 'Asian democracy', which government leaders declared – and many academic and policy analysts seemed to agree – represented an alternative to the ascendant liberal democratic model.

Instead, we are writing this in the late 2010s. The old issues have not disappeared, but are much less salient. The present reality is characterised by a curious blend of strong states and vibrant and penetrating markets; by media that are in structural transition, as journalistic organisations struggle to stay afloat even as audiences swim in increasingly vast digital media options. Democracy is on the defensive, with even the Western powers that once gallantly tried to export it to Southeast Asia now suffering what has been called a democratic recession or deconsolidation (Diamond, 2015; Foa & Mounk, 2017). The economic order, shaped for at least two decades by neoliberal market fetishism, lumbers on despite its patent inability to deliver social justice and environmental sustainability (Jomo, 2016; Mishra, 2017). Our perspective is influenced by these uncertain times.

No doubt, Southeast Asia has undergone profoundly positive changes in the space of a generation. Around eight out of every ten of its adults now get to pick their leaders in more-or-less competitive elections. In every country, media choice has proliferated thanks to television and the Internet. It has become harder for despots to hide wrongdoing or quash dissent. More than ever before, today's Southeast Asians expect the powerful to be accountable, and the weak to have a voice. But these raised expectations also demand that we examine critically media trends in the region. The media's democratic potential remains unfulfilled. This is not only because of direct coercion by governments – the traditional object of analysis when studying media and power. The core argument running through the following sections is that the development of free, independent, and plural media has been complicated by trends towards commercialisation, digital platforms, and identity-based politics. These have interacted with state power in complex ways, opening up political space and pluralising discourse, but without necessarily resulting in structural change.

We flesh out our argument using Southeast Asian case studies. Section 2 looks at media in democratic transitions, with a focus on Indonesia, Myanmar, and Malaysia. Section 3 examines Singapore as an important case of authoritarian resilience. Section 4 surveys the political economy of media in the region's non-communist societies, including Cambodia, Indonesia, Malaysia, Myanmar, the Philippines, and Thailand. Section 5 turns to the topic of intolerance and hate speech in Myanmar and Indonesia. Section 6 studies the Internet's impact on Vietnam and Malaysia and offers concluding thoughts.

We apply and extend insights from media studies to our chosen cases, which we describe in some detail for the sake of readers who are unfamiliar with these societies. We thus hope to provide a conceptually as well as contextually rich account of media and power in the region. That having been said, we do not try to provide a comprehensive survey of Southeast Asia's eleven nation-states and their media. We have selected countries that illustrate our chosen themes best – and that we know better. We focus on journalism, including so-called citizen reporting and blogs, and other informational and political media such as books and documentary films where relevant. We do not deal with popular media, which we acknowledge have an underappreciated impact on political culture and values.

We should declare here our position as writers. While our study is evidence-based and guided by disciplinary concerns, neither of us can be described as detached or disinterested scholars. We are ourselves citizens of Southeast Asian – of Singapore and Malaysia – and have spent most of our adult lives advocating for more democracy and media freedom in our own countries and beyond. We view media as a powerful set of institutions and practices that have emancipatory and civilising potential but tend to be captured and corrupted by powerful interests for their own ends – often in ways that are not immediately obvious, but that critical scholarship can help reveal.

This normative thrust is aligned with international human rights principles, as articulated by Frank La Rue, who took a special interest in Southeast Asia during his tenure as the United Nations' special rapporteur on freedom of expression (2008–14). Journalism, he noted in one of his annual reports to the UN, 'must be seen as an activity and profession that constitutes a necessary service for any society, as it provides individuals and society as a whole with the necessary information to allow them to develop their own thoughts and to freely draw their own conclusions and opinions'; this is a right that enables people to 'make informed decisions and express their opinions freely and participate actively in a democratic system' (UN Human Rights Council, 2012: 3).

Our approach is also informed by the multidimensional conceptualisation of media development adopted by UNESCO – the UN Educational, Scientific, and Cultural Organization – in 1991. For media to fulfill their social role, it is not enough that they be free from illegitimate restrictions by the state. They must also be sufficiently independent from political and commercial pressures to allow them to exercise professional standards and ethical decision-making. There also must be a plurality of media to ensure that diverse perspectives and interests are represented in the national conversation. More recently, the safety of journalists and other communicators has been recognised as yet another distinctive component of freedom of expression as it pertains to media. Thus, media freedom, independence, pluralism, and safety are the key benchmarks that we apply in this study (UNESCO, 2018a).

1.1 Media Freedom, Independence, Pluralism, and Safety

Southeast Asia is one of the most politically diverse regions in the world. In 2019, its eleven nations included two of the world's five remaining communist regimes (Laos and Vietnam); one of the handful of absolute monarchies (Brunei); two democracies with vibrant and competitive polities (Indonesia and the Philippines); two others stifled by the military (Myanmar and Thailand); one rated free but fragile (Timor-Leste); another, once free but now broken (Cambodia); and two of the world's longest-lasting electoral authoritarian regimes – one recently ousted (Malaysia) and the other still going strong (Singapore).

As for press freedom, Southeast Asia's media systems are global under-performers. None is rated as 'free' according to Freedom House, which conducts the most comprehensive annual assessments of this kind. None has a press freedom score that places it in the world's top one-third. Other than Timor-Leste, the Philippines, and Indonesia, all are in the bottom 25 per cent (Freedom House, 2017). Press freedom indices are crude measures that may conceal significant details. For example, although Singapore, Malaysia, and Cambodia were rated within three points of one another on Freedom House's 100-point scale, they are unfree in markedly different ways. Wealthy Singapore's regime is the most hegemonic of the three but also the safest for journalists. Upper-middle-income Malaysia has the strongest civil society movement for media freedom. Lower-middle-income Cambodia's media system is the most corrupt and the most exposed to arbitrary coercion. Such differences matter for social scientific prediction as well as for advocacy and activism. They point to different regime strengths and vulnerabilities, and different opportunities and threats for agents of democratic change.

All Southeast Asian countries have laws that are incompatible with the right to freedom of expression. These include discretionary newspaper licensing laws, which allow governments to suspend or terminate a publication at will – or, for that matter, to never let it start. Singapore uses this power to protect the monopoly of its pro-government publishing behemoth, Singapore Press Holdings. The Malaysian government suspended the financial newspapers of The Edge group for three months in 2015 to block its reporting of the massive corruption scandal concerning the state investment fund, 1MDB. (The suspension was set aside by the High Court after two months.) Defamation laws are also problematic. Defamation is universally regarded as a legitimate limitation on free speech – if treated as a civil matter. But criminal defamation is on the books in several countries and has been actively used in Cambodia, Myanmar, and Thailand. States also restrict media freedom with sweeping and vaguely worded laws policing national security and insult. These include blasphemy law in Indonesia, Malaysia, and Myanmar, and lèse majesté in Thailand.

While media *freedom* from government control is constrained by a range of repressive laws, the main threats to media *independence* arise from news organisations' ownership structures and commercial orientations. All media owners need to keep an eye on the financial bottom line, but they vary in their commitment to protect journalism's public service mission from market pressures. Most news organisations have cut manpower budgets and required editorial decision-making to become more advertiser-friendly. As a result, media have become more consumer-oriented, emphasising lifestyle and entertainment at the expense of news and information required for the country's civic health. Furthermore, many owners treat their media outlets as vehicles to promote their own business and political interests. This tendency is particularly serious in Indonesia, where some major media outlets are turned into barely camouflaged campaign vehicles during election season.

Commercial pressures are a universal problem that cannot be eliminated; but they can be mitigated by a strong professional ethos at the organisational and national levels, cultivated by educational and training institutions, journalism associations, independent press councils, media monitoring civic groups, and other accountability mechanisms. Such organizations can help push back against commercial forces. Unfortunately, the foundations for professionalism in Southeast Asian media are generally undeveloped. They are probably strongest in the Philippines and Indonesia, but even there, their influence is limited to a few higher-quality media outlets.

Media *pluralism* has increased over the decades, spurred by economic and technological progress. More and more Southeast Asians have joined the ranks of the consuming classes that media companies and advertisers want to reach, resulting in the mushrooming of media serving different demographic segments, geographic regions, and cultural niches. For example, Malaysia's successful *Sinar Harian* chain of newspapers, launched in 2006, provides local coverage complementing the national dailies. Radio, with its lower financial barrier to entry as well as its accessibility to rural audiences, contributes significantly to media pluralism. Thailand in particular has a lively community radio sector, comprising several thousand small stations of varying quality. Cambodia was also notable for its many independent radio stations – thirty-two of which were apparently so effective in circulating alternative viewpoints that they were shut down in a pre-election sweep by the government in 2018.

The most hospitable medium for plural voices is the Internet, at least for people who are digitally connected. Several mainstream outlets in the region, such as the Philippines' ABS-CBN network, have harnessed the new opportunities of multimedia storytelling and citizen reporting, thus raising the quality and quantity of previously neglected grassroots perspectives. Being less capital-intensive and more loosely regulated than print and broadcast media, the Internet has also enabled new players to challenge mainstream media organisations and the state's hegemony over media. Around half of Southeast Asia's population count as internet users, with penetration rates ranging from around one-third in East Timor, Laos, and Myanmar; half in Indonesia; two-thirds in the Philippines and Vietnam; and four-fifths in Malaysia, Singapore, and Thailand (Kemp, 2018). Such data are difficult to interpret. Not all internet use has any relevance to public affairs or political discourse, so high penetration may not translate into more plural politics; conversely, though, penetration rates may underestimate the Internet's impact in periods of heightened interest in politics, such as during elections, when online content tends to be eagerly shared by word of mouth or hardcopy printouts (George, 2006).

One way to think about pluralism is in terms of the access that diverse communities have to media, both as producers and as consumers. It is in this respect that media pluralism in Southeast Asia has grown. But another measure of pluralism is the range of relevant voices heard by the general public on matters of common concern. In this regard, media pluralism in the region is lacking. In many countries, alternative viewpoints are pushed to the fringe. Even if they are not completely silenced, they are excluded from engaging in mainstream debates. Political polarisation means that media consumption occurs in silos, with little dialogue across ideological or cultural boundaries.

Public service broadcasting – mandated to facilitate such dialogue in Western Europe, Canada, and Australia – is weak in Southeast Asia.

As for media *safety*, the 2009 Maguindanao massacre in the Philippines remains the single deadliest attack on journalists in world history. Thirty-two media workers were among the fifty-eight individuals slaughtered in this election-related killing spree. The immediate shock at the murder has been replaced by lingering outrage at the perpetrators' impunity. A local political clan, aided by police and militiamen, has been accused of the murder, but as the tenth anniversary of the event approached, there were still no convictions. In the decade from 2007, a total of eighty journalists were killed in the line of duty in Southeast Asia, mostly in the Philippines, but also in Cambodia, Indonesia, Myanmar, Thailand, and Vietnam (UNESCO, 2018b). Body counts underestimate the safety problem. Intimidation, including harassment of female journalists, can constrain the media even if it does not materialise in physical violence. Incitement to hatred against journalists is part of the authoritarian populist toolkit used by leaders such as Rodrigo Duterte of the Philippines.

1.2 Media Organisations

Similar to those of other regions, Southeast Asia's news media come in diverse organisational forms and formats. The digital revolution has encouraged convergence, such that newspapers now also produce video, while television news channels also publish text, for example. It has also been highly disruptive, with several traditional news media platforms losing attention, influence, and profits. In Singapore's relatively mature media market, total print newspaper circulation shrank by 15 per cent between 2012 and 2016. At the same time, it grew by more than 25 per cent in Indonesia (Campbell, 2017). On the whole, legacy media organisations are stronger than digital-born outlets in terms of their capacity for news gathering and their branding and marketing muscle. Therefore, in each country, the biggest online news and information players tend to include the digital operations of established newspapers, such as *Kompas* in Indonesia, *The Star* in Malaysia, *The Straits Times* in Singapore, and the *Philippine Daily Inquirer*.

Television news markets are highly competitive in Indonesia, Thailand, and the Philippines. Myanmar opened up the domestic TV news market to private companies in 2018. In most of the region, though, states have been reluctant to loosen their hold on broadcast news. In Malaysia, the government broadcaster conceded its monopoly in the 1980s – but to a station owned by the ruling party. In Cambodia, similarly, competition among TV channels does not amount to meaningful pluralism since the main ones are all run by government members or businessmen linked to the ruling party. In communist Laos and Vietnam, and in the absolute monarchy of Brunei, the national broadcaster monopolises domestic services, functioning as an undisguised mouthpiece of the people in power. Singapore's MediaCorp (which includes its external service, Channel NewsAsia) is also a monopoly provider of national TV news. Although structured like a commercial entity and manifesting strong production values, it takes instructions from government officials.

There is no strong tradition of independent public service broadcasting in Asia. Indonesia's state networks, TVRI and RRI, were promised a makeover into independent public service media, but this has been delayed by political bickering. As a result, Indonesian TV is highly polarised, with stations aligned with the economic and political interests of their owners. The Thai Public Broadcasting Service, set up in 2008, was mandated to serve the public interest without political interference, but politicians unhappy with its coverage have repeatedly threatened its funding. The Philippines, perhaps because of its American-influenced political system, did not create a state-funded broadcaster. In the former British colonies of Malaysia and Singapore, governments did not follow the BBC example but instead claimed they needed direct control of the airwaves to further their urgent economic development and nation-building missions.

Though relatively small, independent online media contribute disproportionately to the region's media pluralism. They tend to provide more critical coverage of public affairs than do mainstream media. Several were launched with the aid of external funding from international media development foundations. The region's most successful independent online media projects include Malaysia's *Malaysiakini* and the Philippines' *Rappler.* Another traditional way media have sought autonomy is to remain outside the national territory of the state. Exile media such as the Democratic Voice of Burma were important sources of news during Myanmar's junta period. Vietnam's large diaspora communities are also significant producers of media. The *Sarawak Report* investigative blog, authored by a Borneo-born journalist based in Britain, was at the forefront of exposing Malaysia's 1MDB scandal.

Compared with media markets in Europe and the Americas, Southeast Asia's are more linguistically divided. English-language titles are the main national newspapers in the Philippines and Singapore, but even in these countries local languages are preferred by television news viewers. In Indonesia and Thailand, English-language newspapers are read mainly by educated urban elites and expatriates. In Malaysia, the widest-circulating newspaper is in neither the national language of Malay nor the urban working language of English but in Chinese, serving the country's largest ethnic minority community. Linguistic divides are usually associated with other important distinctions. Producers working in different languages are often informed by different professional norms and traditions, while their respective audiences may differ in their racial and religious loyalties, social class, and educational levels.

1.3 Norms and Values

Understanding Southeast Asian media requires some conceptual decluttering. The media of the Global South have rarely been studied on their own terms; they are often implicitly viewed in a Eurocentric frame, with Western democratic systems being used as the default yardstick. The resulting essentialised accounts tend to extrapolate from stereotypes of Asian culture or political systems. These habits have infected the widely used concepts 'development journalism' and 'Asian values'.

Development journalism was first articulated in the Philippines in the 1960s as a professional reform movement that called on media in the Global South to resist sensationalism and respond constructively to their countries' pressing socio-economic needs (Romano, 2009). Some governments latched onto the concept to make the case that the press should be their willing partners in nation-building and economic development, thus justifying their authoritarian controls. This was also the case with 'Asian values', a debate that peaked in the 1990s, when the West's democracy-promotion industry was in overdrive following the collapse of the Soviet Union and its satellite states (George, 2019). The slogan had rhetorical utility among Southeast Asian states, particularly Singapore, Malaysia, and Indonesia, which were resisting Western-style liberal democracy and press freedom. They argued that their own civilisational values – social harmony, order, communitarianism, and respect for authority – were national strengths, as demonstrated by their high levels of economic growth.

Many journalists and scholars adopted the concept, even though its flaws were fairly obvious. Asian values, as set out by its self-styled spokesmen, actually described Confucian societies at most, and even then only superficially – since even China had a long tradition of dissent and revolt. Government leaders stopped using the slogan after the late 1990s, when the Asian Financial Crisis made the old rhetoric ring hollow. Furthermore, democratic transitions in Indonesia, South Korea, and Taiwan debunked the theory that Asians had no cultural appetite for freedom. Pro-democracy protest movements in Malaysia and Myanmar took longer to bear fruit but made the same point.

Many of the earlier claims made about Asian media were based on what Asian leaders said about them. It was simplistically assumed that in authoritarian settings, media workers had no agency – perhaps even no minds of their own – and that the media uncritically internalised official positions or national cultures. Fortunately, more recent studies have taken the trouble to ask journalists themselves about their values and norms, either through detailed surveys or ethnographic research. The multi-country *Worlds of Journalism* study, for example, reveal that each country has not one but several co-existing professional subcultures. In Indonesia, the Southeast Asian country included in the study, around half of the journalists surveyed identified with the 'opportunist facilitator' role, which sees media as partners of power. But almost four in ten Indonesian journalists saw themselves as having an interventionist, adversarial role as 'critical change agents', compared with only two in ten American journalists. Barely one in ten Indonesians identified themselves as 'detached watchdogs', compared with almost two-thirds of American journalists (Hanitzsch, 2011). Recent multi-country analyses of news content (Mellado et al., 2017) make it even clearer that national or regional media systems are not homogeneous. They are hybrid. Differences within nations – between tabloid-style television news and establishment newspapers, for example – are as important as differences between them.

Qualitative researchers, meanwhile, have helped to correct old stereotypes through their deep dives into the journalistic practices of various Southeast Asian countries. For example, although many governments of Muslim countries are infamously intolerant of press freedom, Steele (2018) has shown that many Muslim journalists in the region who believe in independent, public service journalism view themselves as applying values drawn from their religious teachings. In-depth ethnographic and survey research has tended to cut through the 'container thinking' that treats national territories as the default unit for comparison and categorisation (Couldry & Hepp, 2012).

Any research into Asian media norms must also confront the reality of corruption within the profession. So-called 'envelope' journalism is widespread: due to low salaries, reporters, when they attend media events, expect to be handed packets of cash from newsmakers. In several countries, some investigative reporters are motivated by the opportunity for blackmail: they demand hush money from politicians and businessmen once wrongdoing is detected. Higher ethical standards tend to be promoted by a handful of more principled media organisations, professional associations, and press councils.

1.4 Parsing the Media-and-Democracy Question

The following sections present case studies of democratic transitions and non-transitions, of media commercialisation, identity politics, and internet disruption. They advance our larger argument that developing democratic media requires much more than addressing direct government censorship and coercion. We are circumspect about making any grander claims than that, partly because the sheer diversity of contexts in Southeast Asia defies generalisation.

Besides, the media-and-democracy question is ambiguous and does not lend itself to a single, simple answer. Democratisation could refer to regime change or to changes in the style of governance, improved public access to information and ideas, wider and deeper citizen participation, or a transformation in political culture. Rarely do these all occur at once, but in every Southeast Asian country there has been movement along some of these dimensions while others remain stubbornly resistant to progress.

Our analysis is open to all these ways of thinking about media and power but leans toward the idea of participation. This is in line with the theoretical framework adopted by Hansson and Weiss (2018) in their study of political participation in Asia. They deploy the concept of 'political space' to refer to something broader than state arenas or formal institutions. It is 'a multidimensional arena for empowerment at the level of ideas as well as policies or other instrumental objectives, and working with, against, or around fellow citizens as well as the state' (p. 6). It allows for 'a wider conception of political participation, beyond procedural and formal definitions centred around transfer of political authority from citizens to officials through elections, and as exercised by both formal and informal actors' (p. 8). They conceptualise political space as a realm of struggle, where different and unequal groups – including members of political, economic, and civil society, and with pro-democratic and anti-democratic tendencies – try to expand or constrict boundaries and modes of engagement to suit their interests. We explore the media's role in these struggles, starting in the next section with the dramatic political changes that have occurred in Indonesia, Myanmar, and Malaysia.

2 Media and Democratic Transitions

On 9 May 2018, Malaysians voted out the Barisan Nasional (BN), which had governed the country since independence in 1957, and elected a four-party coalition led by a former prime minister, Mahathir Mohamad. With this dramatic change came a chance for reforms in media and free expression. The new Pakatan Harapan government had made campaign promises to repeal repressive laws and create a freer environment for media. The election result was greeted with scenes of jubilation at independent news outlet *Malaysiakini*. 'We think *Malaysiakini* can do better in a business environment that is friendlier to independent media,' said its editor-in-chief Steven Gan (interview, 1 June 2018). 'At the same time, we face more competition with more players joining the fray, but competition is good for news consumers.' But some were skeptical about whether establishment media could shed the habit of toeing the line set by whoever was in power. Veteran journalist Zakiah Koya said, 'The seniors would find it difficult to change their mentality, and therefore there is a likelihood of them just throwing their weight behind Pakatan Harapan as they have done for BN' (interview, 1 June 2018).

These mixed sentiments are symptomatic of some of the uncertainties that arise when an authoritarian media system loosens up. Reflecting on Indonesia's experience a decade after the collapse of President Suharto's thirty-two-year rule, Sen and Hill's (2011) edited volume highlights the nuances and tensions of post-authoritarian contexts, where the rules and practices of democracy are still being constructed. While the state may recede as a major censor, new forces emerge to constrain the media's ability to exercise their democratic role.

Southeast Asia is fertile ground to study such dynamics. There have been notable cases of authoritarian rule and outright dictatorship being replaced by more-democratic systems. Political changes since the mid-1980s in the Philippines, followed by Thailand and Indonesia, were part of a global wave of democratisation, including media reforms, heralded by the fall of the Iron Curtain (Voltmer, 2013). It would take almost another two decades before Myanmar and Malaysia experienced similar changes. These two countries were viewed pessimistically as 'non-transitions' by democracy scholars in the early 2000s (McCargo, 2003). Myanmar, however, underwent top-down reforms after 2011, when the military junta appointed a quasi-civilian government, which announced a liberalising changes. In Malaysia, citizens ousted the dominant party through the ballot box in 2018. This section focuses on the experiences of these two countries, while also drawing on the case of Indonesia, whose democratic transition through popular mobilisation can be said to have been successfully consolidated.

2.1 Media and Democracy

At the level of broad principle, democracy has near universal appeal as a system of government that is accountable to and chosen by equal citizens. In its detailed application, though, it remains intensely debated. For societies transitioning away from authoritarian rule, there is no agreed-upon road map. There is a long history of foreign consultants pushing institutions and linear processes based on their own favoured contexts. Prescriptions too often overlook democracy-undermining inequalities of wealth and power, which tend to deepen as market-based economies develop (Carpentier, 2011; Whitehead, 2002). Nor do template frameworks adequately address the systematic exclusion of women from decision-making (Cornwall & Goetz, 2005).

Such debates notwithstanding, media clearly have an important role in facilitating and sustaining democratisation (UNESCO, 2008). Media themselves undergo transformations in the course of political transitions. Democratisation requires media reforms to challenge pre-existing media monopolies, address the negative impact of economic liberalisation in the media sector, and increase public access to information and to the means of content production (Price, Rozumilowicz, & Verhulst, 2002). An enabling environment for media is one where the state does not regulate journalists; faces limits on its ownership or control of media; and is restricted in its use of laws on criminal defamation, libel, or sedition, which can impede media work (Price & Krug, 2000). Yet, it is rarely possible to dismantle the old regimes completely. New power holders, including those in the media, tend to negotiate and forge alliances with different factions of the previous regimes on the grounds of ensuring continuity or to prevent power grabs. In his analysis of Pacific Asia, McCargo (2003) notes that the various individuals and organisations making up the media sector respond in different ways to realignments of power and economic resource allocation. They can be agents of stability that work to preserve the social order, or agents of restraint that provide checks and balances on the political order, or agents of change that help shape political changes during times of instability or crisis. Schudson (2011), similarly, suggests that we should not assume that media or journalists are inherently democratic or promote democracy. The media sector can instead be seen as a 'magnifying glass' through which we can understand the achievements and drawbacks of democratisation (Voltmer, 2013).

Reforms are mainly top-down – because of the role that governments, legislators, and international organisations play in enacting or repealing policies – but wider stakeholder participation can significantly impact outcomes (Segura & Waisbord, 2016). Civil society groups often use reform processes to raise public awareness and consciousness about the value and functions of free speech in a democratic society (Price & Krug, 2000). Political openings also give these groups the opportunity to form new alliances, engage the public, and initiate campaigns to repeal problematic legal obstacles. The extent and direction of media reforms also depend on external actors. Funding priorities of Western donors have influenced the course of reforms in Southeast Asia. The 1990s democratic wave saw a boost in financial assistance from Western governments and foundations, which were keen to support media in transitioning societies by building their capacities as watchdogs, replacing state media with independent media and public service broadcasting, and reforming laws affecting media. American state and private foundations allocated over US

$600 million for media development globally, especially after the fall of the Soviet bloc (Hume, 2004), although country- and media-specific data are difficult to obtain. Nevertheless, countries in Asia continue to be major beneficiaries, including Indonesia and Myanmar, which received almost US $82 million and US $52 million respectively between 2010 and 2015 (Meyers & Angaya Juma, 2018).

2.2 Media's Role in Southeast Asian Transitions

The media's contributions to political transitions in Indonesia, Myanmar, and Malaysia are not easy to pin down. For the most part, the pre-transition media were highly restricted, limiting their capacity to communicate dissent and turning them into ready vehicles for their respective regimes' favoured narratives, whether on economic policies, political debates, or social relations. State control, however, was never total. The market orientation of commercial media and a democratic ethos among media professionals meant that there was always some resistance within news organisations to the state's preference for media that served a purely propaganda function. Occasional crackdowns – such as the banning or suspension of publications or arrests of journalists – demonstrated not only the governments' overwhelming power but also the existence of some pushback by media. Media deregulation and privatisation, the adoption of new information and communication technologies, and fractures within the establishment were all factors that opened up space for media practices and content that strayed from official scripts. Even journalists of Myanmar, the most closed of the three regimes, could and did resort to operating in exile. Media responded to such opportunities by pushing the boundaries, and these served to construct alternative or opposing realities for readers and viewers. Even if they did not trigger change themselves, media outlets facilitated the more open political expression needed to tip the country towards democratisation.

In Indonesia, a people's movement led to the fall of Suharto's New Order regime in 1998, setting in motion reforms that made its controlled media freer and more robust, and elevating citizens' freedom of expression as a right to be defended rigorously. The proximate cause of the Reformasi movement was economic, in the form of the 1997 Asian Financial Crisis, which resulted in soaring prices for ordinary Indonesians. Activists note, however, that among the earlier events that helped mobilise opposition to the government was its 1994 ban of three critical magazines, *Tempo, Detik,* and *Editor.* The crackdown compelled journalists, artists, students, and others to confront Indonesia's poor press freedom situation. Media freedom activist Eko Maryadi, who was imprisoned for defying a publication ban, said there was an emerging consensus that freedom of the press and access to information belonged to the public (interview, 8 May 2016). The Reformasi movement championed political freedom, freedom of the press, and the decentralisation of power – ideas that continued to guide both civil society and the new political leaders. Post-Suharto Indonesia set new benchmarks for press freedom and freedom of expression in the region.

The Asian Financial Crisis of 1997 also hit Malaysia, spawning a Reformasi movement there as well. The protests did not produce the same dramatic result as in Indonesia; the transition required a far longer gestation period. Mahathir Mohamad's sacking of Anwar Ibrahim as his deputy prime minister led to the formation of a new political party by the latter's supporters and energised an alternative online media sector. A decade later, pro-democracy activists built a coalition, Bersih, to push for electoral reform and political freedoms. From the first Reformasi demonstrations, it would take 20 years for oppositional and civil society efforts to bear fruit. The tipping point was the unbridled kleptocracy of Najib Abdul Razak, under whose leadership from 2009 to 2018 the Barisan Nasional government was embroiled in a massive financial scandal involving public trust funds, the 1Malaysia Development Berhad (1MDB). Opposition politicians and political activists, together with national, alternative, foreign, and social media, focused international attention on the issue and created the ground swell against the incumbent regime.

Myanmar, one of Asia's most repressive regimes, underwent reforms from 2011. When junta leader Than Shwe announced his retirement early that year and handed over leadership to a nominally civilian leader, Thein Sein, observers and those working in exile were initially taken by surprise. There had been major episodes of protest – most recently an uprising by monks in 2007 – but these were decisively put down. The reforms were the result of backroom dealings rather than open confrontation. From the early 2000s, the military leaders began to understand that it was in their own self-interest to devise an exit strategy, later dubbed the Seven Step Roadmap to Disciplined Democracy, that would preserve their wealth and freedom (Lall, 2016). The groundwork was done by civil society representatives and international donors in private meetings with the junta from around 2005. At the time of the opening, conflicts in the ethnic states were ongoing, and the National League for Democracy (NLD), Aung San Suu Kyi's party, had boycotted the 2010 elections. But international and domestic pressure to open up the political space led to proposals for media reform. Private and exiled media helped to steer the change, especially after Thein Sein declared his belief in free media as the Fourth Estate. The subsequent election of the NLD in 2015 inspired hope for greater openings and freedoms, but the party and its leadership have been criticised for failing to deliver as promised.

2.3 Legal Reforms

A key goal during political transitions is to change the laws that have suppressed the media in the past. In Indonesia, media reform was high on the agenda when Suharto fell. Just one week after the swearing in of the new president, B. J. Habibie, his information minister met with a group of media professionals and activists; he agreed to all of their ten demands (Steele, 2012). The speed with which the opportunity for reform was seized was an indicator of not only the new government's commitment to change, but also the dogged investment in capacity building and thought leadership by the country's besieged liberals and radicals. For example, the four-year-old Alliance of Independent Journalists had not stopped strategising for a new democratic Indonesia even after it was outlawed. Meanwhile, Goenawan Mohamad, editor of the banned *Tempo* and a member of the delegation that visited the information minister, had been running a clandestine support group for dissident journalists, which helped to ensure that professional solidarity and spirit were not totally extinguished by Suharto's media crackdowns (Steele, 2005). Thus, press freedom was secured as one of Reformasi's first and most momentous victories. The Habibie government's new press law removed licensing provisions for the print media, prior censorship, and restrictions on forming associations. It also created an independent press council to replace the government body that functioned as a controlling mechanism in the past. Other laws that directly impacted the media and public access to information were later enacted, such as the Broadcasting Law 2002 and the Public Information Disclosure Act 2008.

In Myanmar, Thein Sein's quasi-civilian government dissolved the Press Scrutiny and Registration Division in 2012. This agency had been responsible for the archaic practice of censoring all print materials prior to publication. The move was one of the first of many steps to improve the legal environment for media. Within three years of the announcement of reforms, two new media laws were put in place – the Media Law, and the Printing and Publishing Enterprise Law. The repeal of the junta-era law dating from 1962 was a significant milestone. For the first time in fifty years, newspapers could print on a daily basis instead of only weekly or monthly and did not need government approval for their content. There has been no political will, however, to tackle other problematic laws that could easily curb expression and media work, among them the Electronic Transactions Law (used in the past against bloggers and activists) and laws on assembly and association. Not coincidentally, Myanmar's journalism profession lacks the organisation and influence of its Indonesian counterpart.

In Malaysia, the Pakatan Harapan government promised in its election manifesto to review laws affecting the media. The list includes the Printing Presses and Publications Act 1984, under which the government licenses publications; and the Sedition Act, which criminalises several types of expression. Pakatan Harapan had also said it would introduce a freedom of information law, and restrictions on political ownership of the media. As of mid-2019 there has been no progress on any of these fronts as well as in many other policy areas. In its first 100 days in office, the Pakatan Harapan (PH) government delivered only three out of the ten key promises made. Frustration has set in, and PH leaders have admitted that their manifesto was too ambitious as they did not expect to win. Nevertheless, the lower house of Parliament's repeal of the sweeping Anti-Fake News Act and the government's plans to ratify international treaties on civil and political rights are among the more positive indications that it is serious about expanding media freedom.

Even if implemented, though, legal reforms may be illusory. Regulations and policies can be abused by the state or designed to benefit old power holders or emerging interest groups (Milton 2001; Peruško 2013). While freedom may be high on transitional societies' wish lists, competing priorities such as order and morality can also have a major impact on lawmaking. Thus, Indonesia's State Intelligence Law, Electronic Information and Transactions Law, and the Pornography Law – all introduced in the democratic era – have constrained freedom of expression and media freedom. Broadcast corporations have effectively lobbied lawmakers to counter civil society's calls for restrictions on media cross-ownership. Senior journalist Luvinia, who lost her job due to corporate pressure, is one of many Indonesian journalists who note that powerful media owners have replaced the state as the main source of control and censorship. 'We have come out of the mouth of the crocodile only to be eaten by the lion," she said (interview, 28 April 2017). Constitutional challenges by domestic and international human rights groups have not been able to topple the 1960s blasphemy law, which is defended by the vigorous and even violent support of hard-line religious groups and Islamist parties.

In Myanmar, the new and more liberal media laws have not stopped the government from applying other laws against journalists, in particular, the Official Secrets Act 1923 and the Telecommunications Law 2014. The use of internet laws is worrying in both Indonesia and Myanmar, where hundreds of activists, journalists, and social media users have been investigated and prosecuted for online criminal defamation over the last decade. Free expression and human rights groups have criticised Myanmar's NLD government for abusing the law to keep its critics silent (Freedom House, 2018a). The new NLD lawmakers refused to make deep amendments to the Telecommunications Law, claiming that strong powers were necessary to deal with what they saw as irresponsible use of the Internet. The government argued that online defamation and hate speech had greater impact than offline expression. *Myanmar Now* editor-in-chief Swe Win, who was charged under the Telecommunications Law, made over thirty court appearances since 2017, which he views as a form of state harassment. He was finally acquitted in July 2019. Like his colleagues and other activists, Swe Win has been disappointed with both the quasi-civilian and NLD governments, which failed to deliver meaningful law reforms (Venkiteswaran, Yin, and Myint Kyaw, 2019). Aung San Suu Kyi's NLD, the vessel of most of Myanmar's democratic hopes, seems unable to resist using repressive media laws to strengthen its power.

Political transitions have done away with some of the most egregious censorship tools, such as prepublication vetting in Myanmar and press licensing in Indonesia. The changes, however, have stopped well short of radical transformations into liberal democratic media systems. The paradigm of top-down control, the lack of antimonopoly or cross-media regulation, insufficient support for alternative journalism, and the continued use of criminal law to punish criticism of powerful interests – whether it is the military in Myanmar or the religious establishment in Indonesia – amount to a legal environment that fails to give adequate support to free, independent, and plural media. Also problematic is a weak judiciary, which offers the media insufficient protection against encroachments on press freedom. In Myanmar, a military lacking in accountability still controls key positions in the government. Myanmar's arrest and jailing of journalists whose exposés involved the military indicate its discomfort with watchdog journalism. In Indonesia, guarantees for press freedom in the Press Law have not stopped security forces from acting with impunity to prevent journalists from covering certain areas or issues. The pro-independence movement in Papua has been used as an excuse to retain tight military control over the area, preventing local and foreign media from reporting without fear. The republic's Alliance of Independent Journalists, AJI, declared the police as enemies of the press in 2017, with more than seventy cases of attacks and assaults against journalists in the course of a year.

2.4 Media Adaptations

The pre-transition news media in the three countries acted largely as agents of stability. They worked within existing restrictions partly to remain in business but also, in many cases, because they supported the regimes. The few privately owned and independent media had to navigate the restrictions carefully. The licensing of publications meant that the governments could shut down media operations arbitrarily. Media that survived and prospered were generally those that had made peace with the status quo. Yet, critical journalism could still be found. Writers and editors in Myanmar used creative ways to circumvent censors and discuss the jailed opposition leader, Aung San Suu Kyi. Independent media in Indonesia and Malaysia published stories that questioned government expenditures and policies, thus acting as agents of restraint.

As political changes set in, the media's position becomes more complex. On the one hand, the newly opened space enables more reportage of official corruption and abuse of power, and the inclusion of more diverse voices. On the other, the independent and pro-democracy media that grow in this space may become defenders of the new status quo, offering to play the role of agents of stability. The picture is further complicated by ownership structures. Even as legal controls relax, state actors may continue to have close business ties with media owners (as discussed in Section 4). Transitions bring with them high expectations for the media to shed their old propaganda role and become more vocal champions of public opinion and the public interest. During Malaysia's 2018 election campaign, establishment media outlets were blatantly pro-Barisan, amplifying ruling party voices and virtually blacking out coverage of opposition rallies. But as soon as indications were clear on election night that BN would lose, some immediately shifted the tone of their coverage in favour of the presumptive winners. After the polls, before the new administration was sworn in, even state media started interviewing critics of the BN government. The status of most of the privately held newspapers was even more uncertain. While Malaysia's media laws were now in the hands of the new Pakatan Harapan government, ownership of the major newspapers was still directly or indirectly in the hands of BN political parties. This contradiction could not be resolved quickly. In the months following the election, it was unclear whether the private news media companies could or would strive for editorial independence, or if they would remain in their comfort zone of being partisan and pro-government. In an interview, an editor with a private broadcaster said his media outlet's position in this new environment was to support Pakatan Harapan in pushing the reform agenda. Journalists in the national wire service, Bernama, and other private media outlets described their work as 'business as usual', in other words, serving the government of the day.

As will be discussed in detail in Section 5, the press should not be measured only by how well it plays its government watchdog role. The media's democratic functions include serving as a forum for social conciliation and speaking up for the voiceless in society. To put it another way, the issue of democratic transitions begs the question, transition for whom? In the internally diverse and unequal nations of Southeast Asia, the media constantly confront the challenge of reporting fairly on controversies relating to religion, ethnic identities, discrimination, and human rights abuses. While the media's increased freedom from government control is rightly celebrated, there are worrying signs that journalists in these transitional societies are not as committed as they should be to the principle of equal human rights for all. Thus, many Myanmar newspapers reject the Rohingya identity and have criticised international coverage of the crisis in northern Rakhine State as being too sympathetic towards the community. The hard-line anti-Rohingya stance is found not only in state media such as the *Global New Light of Myanmar*, but even in *The Irrawaddy*, a former exile media with a deserved reputation as a champion of democracy. In Indonesia, a 2009 survey of 600 journalists conducted by Pantau Foundation showed that most were supportive of Islamic fundamentalism, including an edict issued against liberalism and pluralism (Jakarta Post, 2011). The need for civic education for journalists persists long after they gain freedom through media law reform.

2.4.1 Role of Civil Society

The experiences of Indonesia, Myanmar, and Malaysia also show that broad-based civil society coalitions can have a vital role in reforming the media sector in line with democratic transitions. Such movements have been successful in presenting draft legislation or amendments to law, and in campaigning for the expansion of civil liberties including freedom of expression. Since the end of military rule in Myanmar, media professionals have been more vocal in their defence of press freedom, with journalist associations coming together to submit proposals and recommendations on draft media laws and to organise public protests. One of their challenges was to overcome the mutual suspicion between civil society and media, which had been fueled by the military junta over many decades. Civil society activists returning from exile found coalition building a slow process. Nevertheless, the transition provided opportunities for civil society groups, many of which received international support, to come together on issues related to peace, press freedom, and freedom of expression. More than twenty rights groups and journalists' associations formed a coalition in late 2016 to press for changes in the Telecommunications Law, with some success. The coalition also campaigned for the release of individuals imprisoned for expressing their views. Such actions were unthinkable pre-transition, and civil society and independent journalists still have to tread carefully when dealing with criticism of the state institutions.

In Indonesia, civil society was deeply involved in the enactment of the Press Law, the formation of a network of community radio stations, and ensuring legal guarantees for community broadcasters apart from the public and private ones. The country's freedom of information law, known as the Public Information Disclosure Act, was the result of an eight-year campaign involving a wide range of stakeholders under the umbrella of the Koalisi Kebebasan Memperoleh Informasi Publik (Coalition for Freedom of Public Information). The coalition worked with the media to create public awareness and to pressure legislators to support the draft law, which was adopted in 2008. Indonesia is also home to an exemplary multi-stakeholder NGO dedicated to combatting online disinformation, Mafindo (Masyarakat Anti Fitnah Indonesia, or the Indonesian Anti-Hoax Community). Mafindo, together with journalists from major news outlets, were at the forefront of efforts to counter disinformation campaigns that threatened to subvert the 2019 elections. Its extensive citizen-run programmes stand in stark contrast to government-led efforts in Singapore, Malaysia, and elsewhere, which focus on criminal law. It illustrates the kind of civic impulse – a habit of seeking bottom-up solutions to societal problems – that is required to consolidate democracy and protect media freedoms.

One of the key lessons from Indonesia's experience with democratisation is the need to maintain momentum beyond the initial reform period. Civil society groups found it hard to sustain their work. When it became clear that the government was on a democratisation path, international aid institutions shifted funding away from civil society towards strengthening the state. Fatigue among civil society actors was not uncommon. Many activists and journalists opted for more stable jobs in the government administration or private corporations. Such developments reduced civil society's watchdog capacity over powerful interests such as big corporations. Seasoned activists who had championed digital media as a way to increase public participation have been disappointed with how those new channels are now largely in the hands of private companies.

Although at different stages of democratisation, Indonesia, Myanmar, and Malaysia show how media contribute to political change and how they are in turn affected by it. The media in the past worked within the restrictive environments and a state-defined ethos of development journalism. Most of the media, prior to the openings, functioned as agents of stability, although a few tried to serve as checks on the powerful regimes, at great risk to themselves. At the point of transition – whether produced by a people's movement in Indonesia, the self-preservation strategy of the military in Myanmar, or elite splits over corruption in Malaysia – media reforms were recognised as crucial for democratisation. The impetus for reform had different emphases in the three countries. The enlargement of press freedom was central to Myanmar's political transition plan, and one of the early gains in Indonesia's Reformasi agenda. In all three countries, among the salient tasks in reforming the environment for media was to liberalise the laws. This was in line with reformists' assumptions about the important role of the Fourth Estate, and to support the new regime's reform agenda. This process, however, tended to overlook – or was helpless to transform – other structural impediments to democratic discourse, whether in the form of overly partisan and commercially driven ownership, or the systematic exclusion of marginalised groups that are seeking representation and voice in mainstream debates. In all three countries, the initial euphoria of a democratising moment was quickly replaced by an interminable period of reform and consolidation, against powerful political and business interests that tried to capture the media for private gain. Transition has proven to be a marathon and not a sprint.

3 Authoritarian Resilience and Media

Southeast Asia is home to one of the world's most enduring electoral authoritarian regimes: Singapore has held multiparty elections regularly since gaining independence from colonial rule but has never undergone a turnover of government. The People's Action Party (PAP) has governed without interruption since 1959. It poses an enigma for those who assume that authoritarian regimes are inherently unstable and destined to converge with liberal democracies. This section tries to understand the resilience of the PAP by studying its management of the media. Control of the media is one of the standard means of constraining democratic choice and preserving the status quo. The PAP, however, has not engaged in indiscriminately brutal, totalitarian repression of the media. On the contrary, it has preserved power through selective liberalisation and self-restraint in its use of coercion.

This section cautions against binary thinking when studying media and power. States do not work with a single on–off switch that toggles between exposing their countries to the bright light of freedom and condemning them to the dark of despotism. In between are many intermediate phases, where most countries find themselves. According to the 2017 press freedom ratings of Freedom House, 33 per cent of countries were in the 'not free' category, down from 55 per cent three decades earlier. But the 'free' category didn't see commensurate growth. For every one country that achieved press freedom over that period, two entered the 'partly free' box. A plurality of 36 per cent of countries is found in this middle, hybrid category, up from a third-place 21 per cent in 1986 (Freedom House, 2017). Furthermore, even countries that are squarely authoritarian, such as China, exhibit a pragmatic flexibility that does not conform to the totalitarian ideal type, and that may help explain their regime's longevity.

The idea of authoritarian resilience is at odds with conventional liberal wisdom, according to which media freedom doesn't have only intrinsic worth but also instrumental value: it is supposed to make societies stronger. When people are free to explore their options, to construct and express their interests and preferences, and to monitor the performance of officials, there is a greater chance that political power will be exercised in line with their will (Garton Ash, 2016; Norris & Odugbemi, 2010; Oster, 2015). Choking the free circulation of information and ideas can suffocate not only the public and opposition, but also the governing regime itself. Furthermore, watchdog journalism by independent media helps fight potentially destabilising corruption. Seven countries ranked as the top ten cleanest (Transparency International, 2017) are also in the top ten in press freedom (Freedom House, 2017).

Yet, Singapore has managed to combine illiberal politics with sustained high performance on many social and economic indicators. The United Nations' Human Development Index which tracks income per capita plus education and health indicators, ranks Singapore among the world's top ten countries (UNDP, 2018). In Transparency International's corruption perception index, nine of the top ten have a free press; the only exception is Singapore, whose Freedom House press freedom rank is below 150. The PAP has maintained its grip on power despite lower levels of coercion compared with decades past. In the republic's twelve general elections up to 2015, the PAP's share of Parliament seats has not gone below 90 per cent, while its share of the national vote has never dipped below 60 per cent. A closer look at its media system helps to explain how the PAP has managed to have its cake and eat it too.

3.1 Singapore's Media System

Singapore's news media industry is duopolistic, dominated by Singapore Press Holdings (SPH) and MediaCorp. SPH, a public-listed corporation that is closely supervised though not owned by the government, owns all the local daily newspapers, including the flagship *Straits Times*. MediaCorp, wholly owned by the government, runs all the country's free-to-air television channels and most of the radio stations. Independent online news media are underdeveloped, even compared with neighbouring countries that have much lower internet penetration.

The government's most feared legal weapon is the Internal Security Act, which allows arrest without warrant and detention without trial. From 1965 to 2010, around 640 individuals were detained under the ISA, mostly in the earlier decades of this period. They included several working for mainstream news organisations. The biggest ISA crackdown on media was against the country's largest Chinese-language daily, *Nanyang Siang Pau*, which was challenging the government's pro-English language policies. Four of its executives were arrested in 1971. Its publisher was arrested in 1973 and detained for five years. In 1977, two Singaporean writers for the regional magazine, *Far Eastern Economic Review*, were detained for several weeks for allegedly using their articles to promote communism.

Another draconian power is press licensing. Since colonial times, any would-be publisher has had to apply for an annual newspaper licence. The law allows the information minister to reject an application or revoke a permit at any time, effectively banning the publication. Maximum penalties for non-compliance are a two-year jail term and a fine of $50,000. In 1969, the Malay-language *Utusan Melayu* was banned for allegedly inciting racial animosities. In 1971, around the same time that *Nanyang Siang Pau* was under attack, the government revoked the licence of the English-language *Singapore Herald*.

The government is also able to count on other sweeping laws that deter critical journalism. Singapore's defamation, contempt of court, and official secrets laws did not follow the late twentieth-century trend in democratic societies to provide more protection for journalism in the public interest. The lack of any freedom of information law, plus a monolithic and cohesive state machinery that is not prone to leaks, make it even harder for journalists to exercise a Fourth Estate role. More successfully than its counterparts in the rest of non-communist Southeast Asia, the Singapore government transformed the press from a diverse set of players that included adversarial newspapers into a solidly pro-establishment institution.

Singapore is usually placed in the bottom one-quarter in international press freedom rankings. But to understand the system's resilience, we need to look beyond aggregate ratings and rankings. Press freedom indices are composed of many distinct measures – such as the number of attacks on media workers, the existence of right to information laws, and whether regulatory agencies are independent of political control. This means countries with similarly poor scores may be unfree in very different ways. Bangladesh and Mexico, for example, are in the same region of the table as Singapore; but Bangladesh has several journalists imprisoned for their work, while Mexico is one of the deadliest countries for journalists. In contrast, journalists in Singapore enjoy a high degree of physical safety and are almost never imprisoned. Singapore's low ranking is due instead to licensing systems and other laws that have blocked the emergence of independent media. These differences matter: how media freedom is curtailed, not just whether, has an impact on the regime's legitimacy and its ability to co-opt the media, for example. Restraint in the intensity and breadth of coercive censorship has contributed to the PAP's resilience.

3.2 Calibrated Coercion

Using violence can be counterproductive, robbing a regime of the legitimacy it requires to maintain group cohesion (Arendt, 1970). Flagrant censorship, similarly, can backfire by enhancing the appeal of the forbidden fruit and generating moral outrage around which opponents can mobilise support (Jansen & Martin, 2003). Counter-intuitively, therefore, authoritarian resilience requires strategic self-restraint in the use of force. By calibrating their coercion, states are able to lower the costs associated with more draconian measures (George, 2007). Singapore's press controls have evolved along these lines, away from more spectacular measures such as imprisoning journalists and closing down publications, and towards backroom controls as well as economic carrots and sticks that encourage self-censorship.

Although licensing remains in operation, 1971 marked the last time that the PAP used it to close down a daily newspaper. It has not activated detention without trial as an instrument of media regulation since 1977. Instead, the PAP has turned the mainstream press into a compliant institution through unique provisions within the Newspaper and Printing Presses Act (NPPA). Enacted in 1974, the NPPA retained legacy licensing rules but also introduced radical new measures. It says newspapers can be published in Singapore only by public-listed companies. Furthermore, no shareholder can control 12 per cent or more of a newspaper company. The NPPA thus spread newspaper ownership thinly across the stock market, sparing the government the trouble of dealing with the kind of headstrong family owners who had controlled *Nanyang Siang Pau.* Decades later, media scholars would observe that a family that invests its reputation and social capital into a news organisation may develop strong non-pecuniary interests in protecting editorial integrity and professionalism (Ellis, 2014). The PAP was probably the first authoritarian regime to design media policy around this insight. It appreciated that newspaper companies' commercial logic was not necessarily a political threat, and indeed could be used to neutralise the ideological or partisan goals of individual or family publishers.

The PAP's approach differed from most postcolonial authoritarian regimes, which believed they needed to nationalise ownership in order bring the press to heel. To guarantee that newspaper companies do not stray, the NPPA also empowers the government to name their board of directors. Newspaper companies must designate certain shares as 'management shares', which have 200 times the voting power of ordinary shares on any resolution relating to the appointment or dismissal of a director or any member of the staff. The government gets to decide which shareholders possess this supervoting status. SPH management shareholders are typically financial institutions deeply invested in Singapore's political stability.

Through the NPPA, the PAP government gained control over key appointments in Singapore's newspapers. Since 1982, the chairman's seat in the Straits Times group and its successor, SPH, has been occupied by a string of trusted former government officials, including three retired cabinet ministers. Former civil servants were appointed as SPH chief executive officers from 1995. Chief editors are experienced journalists drawn from the newsrooms, but only with the assent of the government.

Much of the time, rank-and-file journalists are able to do their jobs according to global professional norms. Externally imposed political considerations tend to be internalised by senior editors. The resulting editorial decisions, consistently government-leaning on controversial issues, are outwardly defended as the outcome of professional judgment. The rewards for pragmatic acquiescence are considerable. SPH's monopoly profits – a benefit arising from the market protection accorded by government licensing – have enriched not only major shareholders and directors but also senior editors.

The PAP's system gives the national media more latitude than official party mouthpieces such as China's *People's Daily*. As a result, the media occasionally cross the line of politically acceptability, requiring the government to roll out its more coercive weapons. In 1991, an SPH newspaper was fined under the Singapore Armed Forces Act for publishing details about a helicopter crash that it obtained from sources without approval. Two senior SPH journalists were convicted and fined under the Official Secrets Act in 1992 for receiving and publishing government economic data prematurely. Under the same law, a reporter was investigated and given an official warning in 2017 for receiving an unauthorised tip-off from a civil servant. Clearly, the PAP's calibration of its coercion is not the result of any ideological conversion to liberal values. It is about trying to exercise just enough repression to get the government's job done, thus minimising the risk of blowback.

The government's regulation of foreign media follows the same logic. Instead of jailing foreign correspondents or banning publications, it applies largely economic disincentives against hard-hitting journalism. Costly defamation suits have been levelled against the *International Herald Tribune* (the precursor of the *International New York Times*), Bloomberg, and others. In addition, the government has used an innovative 1984 amendment to the NPPA to cap the circulation of offshore publications deemed to be interfering in Singapore's domestic politics (in practice, any publication that does not give the government the unedited right of reply to an offending article). Most foreign news publications, including *Time, Wall Street Journal*, and *The Economist*, have suffered this punishment. The government argued that it was not banning these publications but simply stopping commercial news organisations profiting from what it saw as irresponsible journalism. Its assessment of the foreign media's commercial priorities proved largely correct. Foreign news executives value unfettered access to the Singapore market and its convenient location as an Asian hub more than their right to publish financially risky journalism. Over time, foreign news organisations grew more careful in their reporting and commentary on Singapore, despite the absence of any obvious coercion (Rodan, 2004).

Singapore continues to refine its tools for managing media. In 2019, the government introduced the Protection from Online Falsehoods and Manipulation Act, probably the world's most elaborate and far-reaching legislative response to the so-called 'fake news' crisis. The new law was highly controversial, due to the sweeping discretionary powers it placed in the hands of government ministers. Interestingly, one of the points the government raised in the bill's defence was that existing laws already allowed it to take the extreme step of blocking websites; the new law would provide for more calibrated and measured interventions such as correction orders. But this does not mean that the new law will reduce the incidence or effectiveness of censorship. Paradoxically, the older laws' more extreme powers meant they were suited only as weapons of last resort. In contrast, the new law's more calibrated tools may increase the frequency of government intervention in journalism.

3.3 Differential Censorship

If calibrated coercion modulates the intensity of repression, differential censorship moderates its breadth. Intelligent authoritarian regimes try to target their censorship more precisely while freeing up more and more zones within the mediascape. The other side of the coin of differential censorship, selective liberalisation, can help enhance the regime's legitimacy, given that most populations have an appetite for media choice. Liberalisation also creates opportunities to win over business elites who are keen to invest in media industries. Besides, digital communication has made prior censorship extremely costly and impractical, requiring states to redraw the lines between prohibition and permissibility. Resilient authoritarianism therefore allows most media sectors to become 'pluralistic, with high production values and entertaining content', while maintaining 'state or oligarchic control over information on certain political subjects and key sectors of the media' (Puddington, 2017: 6).

Most obviously, regimes discriminate at the level of the individual article or programme, weeding out content they find objectionable. As this approach is cumbersome and labour-intensive, authoritarian governments, including Singapore's, usually find it more efficient to manage media at the level of ownership, using discretionary licensing systems to ensure that organisations are controlled by individuals who can be trusted to institute self-censorship. Singapore also applies different standards to different communication technologies based how regulable they are: the Internet is significantly more open than traditional media. There are several other dimensions along which differential censorship is applied: regulations differ depending on the capabilities of the media organisation, the symbolic stature of the media brand, the genre of the outlet, the likely demographics of the audience, and the language medium used. By and large, regulators are most sensitive about the political content appearing in mainstream news media that draw a mass audience; they are more – but not absolutely – tolerant of media catering to niche audiences, including the business community and educated elites.

A few examples should serve to illustrate how such differentiation works in practice. When the government took the major step of allowing CNN and other international television channels to enter the Singapore market in the early 1990s, it permitted only financial institutions and hotels to install satellite dishes. It explained that these organisations needed better access to satellite news channels if Singapore was to maintain its competitive edge as a financial and business hub. After cable television was introduced for households, the double standard in favour of business audiences remained. The American business channel CNBC was not only welcomed onto Singapore screens but also encouraged to set up its Asian newsroom in the country. On the other hand, neither of the two subscription TV providers (both of which are government-linked) offer Al Jazeera English, whose sharp social and political reporting has irritated the government.

Differential censorship is also evident in the way the government has conceded substantial space for the individual expression of political viewpoints, including satirical humour, while continuing to restrict more organised efforts to inform and mobilise public opinion. This pattern is most clearly demonstrated in Singapore's internet regulations. While Singapore's press freedom situation places it in the bottom one-third of countries, its internet freedom is rated 'partly free', placing it in the 50th percentile (Freedom House, 2018b). The government does not depend on filtering or blocking, and its post-publication punishments target only a handful of cases each year. It has not attempted to stop the proliferation of individual blogs, recognising that random acts of journalism carried out by lone citizen reporters have limited impact on their own. It has tried to discipline some of them with defamation and contempt of court laws but has not imposed prior restraints. Ordinary Singaporeans are allowed to criticise the government on social media with impunity. Biting satire is regularly created by professional bloggers such as Mr Brown, who does not bother to keep his real identity secret. The government has understood that pluralisation of online views as such is not necessarily threatening to PAP dominance. Indeed, online criticism and satire could serve as a safety valve for discontent.

The government intervenes instead when public opinion is organised and channeled into action, usually at the point where it leaves the online space and materialises as, for example, a physical gathering. In the offline world, the government's traditional dominance applies. It can use restrictions on assembly and political funding, as well as its tight grip on institutions normally associated with protest, such as trade unions, universities, and professional groups. It has also taken efforts to prevent news sites from following in the footsteps of Malaysia's *Malaysiakini* and developing teams of full-time professionals with the capacity to challenge the mainstream media's take on events. The government introduced a series of new regulations starting in 2013, banning such start-ups from receiving foreign grants and loans, and regulating local donations.

Selective liberalisation is also apparent in the greater latitude given to local artists compared with the news media and civic groups. Theatre groups, though subject to censorship, enjoy enough space to produce a regular stream of original plays dealing explicitly with issues such as discrimination against gays, racial prejudice, the cult of personality around Lee Kuan Yew, PAP dominance, and censorship itself. Their productions are able to deal with such controversial issues much more critically than news media, probably because theatre is seen as having only a niche following. They are also less constrained than advocacy groups since they are not set up to organise or mobilise whatever sentiments they arouse.

The government may be treating the arts, like social media, as providing a safety valve for pent-up frustrations with Singapore's tightly controlled politics. Free expression in a political system, however, is harder to contain and channel than steam in a machine. The safety valve could end up providing motive power for political change. The strategy of differential censorship depends on the regime's ability to contain liberalisation within the approved domains. Leakage is a constant possibility. For example, the gap between what is available online and what licensed media are permitted to carry puts the self-censorship system under strain. Furthermore, consumers who grow accustomed to competing suppliers offering them options in entertainment and other nonpolitical media may find the state's monopoly on political news and opinion increasingly unsatisfactory.

So far, the strategy appears to have worked for the PAP. It has allowed the middle class to enjoy entertainment and lifestyle options befitting their status as citizens of a First World city. It serves the information needs of one of the world's main financial centres. And it has attracted many global media companies to set up regional headquarters in Singapore, thus largely achieving the media hub ambitions to a degree that critics once considered implausible. At the same time, the government has kept the media terrain tilted decisively in favour of the PAP. PAP media regulation hovers around this authoritarian sweet spot.

3.4 Beyond Singapore

If indeed calibrated coercion and differential censorship are rational strategies for authoritarian regimes seeking to consolidate their power, we would expect states other than Singapore to be attempting the same. Differential censorship is indeed practised widely in Southeast Asia and beyond. Under Malaysia's Barisan Nasional (BN) regime, private enterprises were awarded television licences from the 1980s, but the resulting proliferation of choice was largely confined to entertainment options. There was no move to turn the government-owned national broadcaster, RTM, into an independent public service entity. Local news programming can also be found on TV3 and Astro. But TV3 is owned by Media Prima, which (at the time of writing) is controlled by UMNO, the main party within Barisan. Astro's main owners are billionaire Ananda Krishnan, who has close links to UMNO, and Khazanah, the government's investment arm.

Vietnam's communist government allows foreign channels to comprise up to 30 per cent of the suite of channels on any pay TV service, but free-to-air TV remains the monopoly of the state. Vietnam is a showcase of hierarchically differentiated censorship, a pattern that has also been observed in China: the government allows, and even applauds, press reports on corruption at the local level, while continuing to prohibit scrutiny of the central government. 'Relaxations and crackdowns against the press are purposefully unpredictable and arbitrary, although reporters run a higher risk of reprisals when they publish allegations against high-ranking officials', Cain (2014: 87) notes about Vietnam. Partial liberalisation is partly a concession to the sheer difficulty of suppressing controversial scandals. It also buttresses the communist party's legitimacy as a benevolent institution dedicated to the national interest.

As for calibrated coercion, the growing literature on Chinese censorship reveals a perceptible shift from outright bans towards so-called 'opinion guidance' (Tai,

2014). In Southeast Asia, governments have shifted gradually from direct to indirect methods of media control. In Myanmar, for example, democratic reforms have meant that newspapers no longer need to submit pages to a censorship office for pre-publication vetting. Self-censorship, however, remains a reality, with editors needing to avoid confrontations with the government and military, which could be costly for media owners. State-run organs such as *New Light of Myanmar* are being transformed into more professional and less propagandistic public service media; but they are likely to remain under political supervision. Privately owned media lack the same resources and will find it hard to compete and survive.

But overall, compared with Singapore, authoritarian tendencies in the rest of Southeast Asia have not been as self-restrained. While the PAP government refrained from using detention without trial and newspaper suspensions as a way to discipline mainstream media from the 1970s, Malaysia's BN government continued to do so into the 2000s. Indeed, it is tempting to claim that BN's more overtly repressive style is one reason it proved less resilient than the PAP. Its direct attacks on the press as well as the undisguised propaganda function of government-run television, the Bernama news agency, and party-affiliated newspapers certainly contributed to its loss of legitimacy in the eyes of urbanites, including many journalists. The causal mechanism probably worked the other way as well, however: Malaysia's relatively higher levels of dissent compelled the government to employ more repressive means, which then backfired.

The relationship between calibrated control and authoritarian resilience is best seen as an interactive one, subject to positive feedback loops. In Singapore, it was the successful neutralisation of practically all sources of dissent in the 1960s and 1970s – using considerable force – that then allowed the PAP to shift towards more ideological and indirect modes of control. That in turn enhanced its hegemonic power and made its rule more palatable to citizens, who were thus prepared to acquiesce to, if not positively support, continued PAP domination. In Malaysia, opposition parties and civil society were never flattened the way they were in Singapore. Its federal system, run by an alliance of parties, meant that there were always competing elites and alternative sources of patronage, even when BN was at the heights of its powers. Singapore is geographically small, with a unitary state under a powerful executive branch atop a highly cohesive political party. The PAP is unusual, perhaps even unique, in its capacity to practise calibrated coercion.

3.5 Rethinking Media and Power

The Singapore case challenges the conventional wisdom regarding the relationship between media systems and good governance. It is widely assumed that free, independent, and plural media contribute positively to government responsiveness, socio-economic development, and freedom from corruption. But while the general relationship holds, media autonomy may not be an all-or-nothing factor. It is possible that moderate levels of press freedom, significantly lower than the liberal democratic standard, may be enough to stave off the worst effects of authoritarian rule. Crucially, the regime has invested in functional equivalents of the Fourth Estate. Although Singapore has no investigative journalism to speak of, the state does have a strong internal watchdog in the form of the Corrupt Practices Investigation Bureau. There are occasional corruption scandals, but the PAP has been spared the legitimacy-crushing burden of endemic graft.

Similarly, analysts may have overstated how free a polity needs to be to enjoy economic development. Studying Singapore, Rodan (2004) has noted that the type of transparency that appeals to global capital is distinct from what citizens need to hold their government to account. In practice, most advanced industrial societies score high on both economic transparency and political transparency, which is why analysts rarely unbundle the concept. Singapore is an exception: it is among the top in its economic and institutional transparency, but below average in political transparency (Kaufman & Bellver, 2005).

Differential censorship and calibrated coercion should not be seen as watertight solutions for an authoritarian regime that seeks to sustain its media system. They achieve a dynamic equilibrium that is largely stable at any point of time, but is never totally resistant to pressures and contradictions that require regular recalibration. With each adjustment, the regime may have to reconcile itself to a more plural and contentious political culture. Authoritarian resilience is not about staying frozen in time. On the contrary, it is about proactively responding to changing times in order to preserve the regime's dominance. This is what the PAP appears to have achieved thus far, in part through its media policies.

4 Big Business and Media

Philippines President Rodrigo R. Duterte has gone on the offensive against what he calls dangerous oligarchs and their media, which he says are obstructing his populist agenda. In Indonesia's 2014 presidential elections, tycoons used their media properties to boost their own political ambitions or support candidates they endorsed. Governments in Cambodia, Myanmar, Malaysia, and Thailand kept a tight leash on the media through business cronies as well as repressive laws.

Oligarchs, tycoons, and cronies are terms that regularly come up when news media are discussed in Southeast Asia. The globally observed tendency towards media concentration, combined with rampant neoliberal ideology, has stamped similar ownership patterns in much of the region, differences in political system notwithstanding. The ownership of media in each country, especially news media, is dominated by a small group of individuals and organisations. This section examines patterns of media ownership and their relationship to political power. It surveys six countries that have competitive politics, albeit to varying degrees, and substantial private media: Cambodia, Indonesia, Malaysia, Myanmar, Philippines, and Thailand.

4.1 Political Economy of Media

Media ownership has been the subject of criticism for more than a century. Although journalism was lauded for its democratic role in speaking truth to power, it became clear by the early twentieth century that the media in industrialised nations were becoming powerful institutions in themselves, often accountable to no one other than their wealthy owners. Freedom from government control, therefore, did not guarantee that journalism would be able to fulfil its democratic roles. As noted in Section 1, journalists would also need to enjoy professional independence from other power centres, including their own employers. From the public's perspective, ownership patterns and business strategies affect the availability of diverse and plural content, which is viewed as essential for building and supporting democratic societies.

Therefore, one of the main concerns in studies of the political economy of media is concentration of ownership, or the degree to which a media market is dominated by a small number of producers. A study of media in thirty countries by the International Media Concentration Collaboration project showed that a mere ninety owners control 30 to 50 per cent of the world's major media assets. They are from the state sector (the biggest case being China) and, for private media, institutional asset management firms and individual and family owners (Noam, 2016). The findings are similar to a study of newspaper and television ownership in ninety-seven countries in the early 2000s, which found that most of the largest media firms were owned by the government or private families (Djankov, McLiesh, Nenova, and Shleifer, 2003).

Another key concept is conglomeration, which refers to how corporations acquire or develop operations across multiple media platforms, such as newspapers, television, the Internet, and events. Conglomeration may be pursued for economies of scope – enabling a single newsroom to produce content for multiple platforms, for example – but usually crowds out smaller players. Scholars have cautioned that such trends could significantly limit the voices in the media, reduce the ability of different stakeholders to engage in meaningful debates, and affect the ability of citizens to participate effectively in politics (Bagdikian, 2004; McChesney, 1998). The anticompetitive consequences of conglomeration make such acquisitions a matter of interest to regulators in many countries. Laws prohibiting cross-ownership of newspapers and broadcasters are common, including in jurisdictions with high levels of press freedom. But barriers to conglomeration have been eroded both by the anti-regulation ethos of neoliberalism and by digital convergence, which is gradually rendering the distinction between print and broadcast media obsolete. Furthermore, large media conglomerates are able to influence policy making, thus consolidating their hold on media markets (Schlosberg, 2017; Klimkiewicz, 2009).

Although the most salient distinction in ownership type is between state and private owners, media scholars have observed that different kinds of private ownership have different implications for editorial independence. Traditionally, many leading newspapers were owned by individual or family publishers, for whom the publication was a source of social status and a vehicle for their political ideals, not just a business pursued for profit. Some of the world's most highly regarded newspapers, such as *The New York Times* and *Washington Post* in the United States and *The Hindu* and *Indian Express* in India, were or are in this category. Many media owners today, however, are corporations oriented to growing shareholder value and returns on investment. This can be especially problematic in the case of diversified conglomerates in which the news divisions form a small part of their total portfolios. In such cases, directors and top executives may be insensitive to the need to protect editorial values against commercial interests.

While most of the early research focused on the corporate media in the liberal democracies of North America and western Europe, studies of postcolonial societies and transitional democracies have shown a blurring of the lines between state and private ownership (Downing, 2011; Klimkiewicz, 2009; Thomas & Nain, 2004). Djankov et al. (2003) argued that government-owned media were typically associated with countries that were poorer and more autocratic, and where the levels of civil liberties and access to public interest information were low. Scholars studying media from a political economy perspective, however, are skeptical that either economic development or globalisation necessarily reduces the state's role in media. Where there has been a shift away from total state control to more democratic systems with improved levels of political freedoms, we see countervailing trends of media capture by power elites, with governments and corporations owning or taking over media (Schiffrin, 2017). States continue to regulate and dominate the television markets in many countries (Turner, 2016). Furthermore, the state still plays a large role in licensing and subsidising telecommunication and other digital technologies, and is often a direct investor in such enterprises. Media convergence has altered the relationships between state actors and other stakeholders, but it has not necessarily rendered state institutions less powerful (Flew, 2016). Scholars have also highlighted how supposed liberalisation can be followed by the recapture of media by owners who were closely associated with the old authoritarian regime (Splichal, 2004; Milton, 2001); or the use of financial inducements or outright corruption to bring the media agenda in line with politicians' interests (Besley & Prat, 2006; Schlosberg, 2017).

4.2 Oligarchs, Cronies, and State Patrons in Southeast Asia

Historically, the broadcast media in the region have been owned or linked to states, with government agencies and military running radio and television stations; whereas the print media in non-communist Southeast Asia are mostly privately owned, with varying degrees of freedom from government control (Brooten, 2016; Lewis, 2006; Siriyuvasak, 2001). Privatisation in the 1980s and 1990s paved the way for a boom in commercial broadcast media, initially in Indonesia and Malaysia, and followed by Thailand and Myanmar. The exception was the Philippines, which had private television owners from the late 1950s. Cambodia's economy since the end of the civil war in the early 1990s was dependent on foreign aid as well as investment, allowing for foreign and locally owned newspapers and television stations to set up amid the largely state-dominated media (Marston, 1996). In Myanmar, five decades of military and government control of the media gave way to a relatively freer private media, although these outlets are facing financial difficulties.

The accumulation of power and capital by cronies and oligarchs has featured prominently in the political economy of Southeast Asia (Hadiz, 2013; Hadiz & Robinson, 2005), including in the media sector (Tapsell, 2015; Sudibyo & Patria, 2013, Dhakidae, 1991). Complaints about cronies – usually referring to businessmen favoured by and dependent on political leaders – were common during the Asian Financial Crisis in Indonesia, Thailand, and Malaysia. Protest movements attacked their role in dragging down the economy. Ford et al. (2016) make a distinction between cronies and oligarchs. Oligarchs, like cronies, benefit from state patronage, but they do not share cronies' dependence on particular regimes. Thus, in their study of Myanmar, Ford et al. (2016) note that the country's recent opening up has created a new oligarchic class of business elites quite distinct from the cronies that operated under the military junta for decades. These oligarchs 'may or may not benefit from patronage but ... are sufficiently wealthy and established so as to exercise independent power' (Ford et al., 2016: 32).

4.2.1 Competition and Capture in Indonesia and Philippines

With almost 800 newspapers, 238 television stations, 450 radio stations, and over 43,000 online media in 2018,[1] Indonesia seems like the poster child for media plurality and diversity. Concentration and conglomeration, however, make such numbers deceptive. Merlyna Lim (2012) describes a media landscape dominated by a 'League of Thirteen', comprising the state plus twelve commercial entities. Five years later, Tapsell (2017) put the number at eight as a result of further consolidation. The giants include those that are traditionally media focused – Kompas Gramedia Group and Jawa Pos Group – while others have clear non-media and political ties. Among the owners in the latter category are Golkar party chairman Aburizal Bakri, who owns Visi Media Asia; Nasdem party founder Surya Paloh, who owns Media Group; and Perindo founder Hary Tanoesoedibjo, who owns Media Nusantara Citra (MNC) Group (Dhyatmika, 2014).

Such political links, which are publicly known, have been allegedly used to either suppress negative reportage about the owners and their political and business allies, or to promote particular agendas, especially during the election season. The environmental disaster in 2006 involving an oil and gas company owned by Aburizal Bakrie, who was then welfare minister, is a case in point. He bought a newspaper in the region, which resulted in a shift in editorial direction to one that was favourable to the company (Tapsell, 2010). During the 2014 elections, Indonesian media fueled partisanship, and owners were reported to have interfered in newsroom decisions (Dhyatmika, 2014). Joko Widodo relied on a network of oligarchs and their media to turn him from an outsider into a frontrunner (Tapsell, 2015a). He went on to win the presidential elections. The trend continued in the run-up to the 2019 elections: partisan reporting reflected the political interests of media owners. In the presidential race, media owners issued open support for one candidate over the other, mostly to the advantage of Widodo, who won a second term (Triyono, 2018).

The Philippines has one of the most diverse and free environments for media and a tradition of privately-owned media. Two companies – ABS-CBN and GMA Network – control almost 80 per cent of the television market. Although they do not have direct political party links, the Philippines is similar to Indonesia in that media owners are conglomerates involved in a wide range of businesses, such as telecommunications, power, banking, and financial services. The owners fit the description of oligarchs. The more notable ones are the Lopez family, who own ABS-CBN; the family of the late Emilio T. Yap, who own

[1] Data shared by Alliance for Independent Journalists (Indonesia) Abdul Manan at a public talk on 17 November 2018, Petaling Jaya, Malaysia.

Manila Bulletin; and Manuel V. Pangilinan, who owns TV5 Network. Pangilinan's stake is said to be controlled in turn by an Indonesian tycoon, Anthoni Salim of Salim Group, through a conglomerate registered in the Philippines, First Pacific. Foreign ownership of media is prohibited in the Philippines, and Salim's supposed stake is a sore point for nationalists. Business tycoon Ramon Ang, owner of the San Miguel Corporation, struck a deal to buy over influential *Philippine Daily Inquirer* from the Prieto family, which buckled under intense pressure from the Duterte government in retaliation for the newspaper's critical reporting (Pascual, 2017). Ang is reputedly closer to Duterte.

4.2.2 Backsliding in Thailand and Cambodia

Thailand has long had a vibrant and competitive media environment. The news industry was characterised by extreme partisanship, especially at the height of the conflict between the pro-royalty 'yellow shirts' and the 'red shirts' loyal to Thaksin Shinawatra in the mid to late 2000s. Following the May 2014 military coup, these divides were subsumed by controls over the media and political expression. The military also sought to delegitimise further the influence of the Shinawatra family by co-opting civil society and endorsing the mounting repudiation of democracy as a suitable political system for the country (Bonura, 2015). Another major development has been the introduction of digital broadcasting, which was meant to multiply choice but has had less than impressive results. The licences were expensive – about THB1 billion (approximately US $45 million) for the high-definition channels – but attracted many bids from companies lured by the promise of lucrative earnings, including from traditional print media such as *Thai Rath* and *The Nation*. A total of twenty-four licences were awarded just before the coup. For most of the licencees, the promised profits never materialised. Many of the digital television stations and even their print media parents are being bought up by wealthy family businesses such as the Charoen Siriwattanapakdi family, which owns Thai Beverage (with brands like Chang beer), and the Prasert Prasatthong-osoth family, which owns Bangkok Airways and the second largest network of hospitals in Asia. These two families own directly and indirectly four digital television stations (Tunsarawuth, 2018). With pressure from the military junta and financial challenges, many media outlets have shut down, allowing the market to be dominated by the conglomerates, government, and the military.

In Cambodia, private media, mainly newspapers, began to thrive after the United Nations–led transition in 1993. As in the rest of the region, though, economic liberalisation did not mean political liberalisation. The government shut down critical media outlets and threatened their owners. In 2018, eight out of the ten television stations belonged to owners politically affiliated with the government of Prime Minister Hun Sen (CCIM & RSF, 2017). The prime minister's daughter, Hun Mana, is one of the two media moguls in the country. She owns Bayon Media Hight System, which broadcasts via three television stations and runs Bayon radio. She is also the owner of the *Kampuchea Thmey Daily*, which together with the broadcast stations, supports the ruling Cambodia People's Party.

In 2017, the government shut down nineteen radio stations such as the Voice of Democracy (VOD), allegedly for breaching their contracts. This cut access to broadcasts by Voice of America and Radio Free Asia, which had been important sources of independent information. The move was seen as part of the government's crackdown on critical voices ahead of the 2018 elections, which also included shutting down the opposition political party (the Cambodia National Rescue Party) and jailing activists. Two independent English-language newspapers were slapped with accusations of tax evasion, resulting in the closure of *Cambodia Daily* and the sale of *Phnom Penh Post* to a Malaysian investor with ties to the prime minister. These English-language titles did not have a large local reader base, but were influential within the economically vital foreign community. Hun Sen's attacks on the media and the opposition, after more than thirty years in power, represented one of the world's severest cases of democratic backsliding in recent years. His government has been impervious to criticism from Western governments and human rights groups, perhaps because of the backing it enjoys from China. Even as the West's media footprint in Cambodia shrinks, China's has been growing. In 2017, a Chinese company, NICE Culture Investment Group, entered into a joint venture with Cambodia's Interior Ministry to set up NICE TV channel, based on the ministry premises.

4.2.3 Overcoming Cronyism in Malaysia and Myanmar

For decades, the national media in Malaysia served the interests of the Barisan Nasional (BN) government. Whether through direct ownership or patronage politics, the component parties of the ruling alliance had a strong grip on the media's editorial direction. Being in government, they also had ready access to repressive laws that could be used to discipline errant media and discourage independent and critical journalism. This ensured media content that reinforced its political hegemony (Nain & Wang, 2004). The ouster of BN in the May 2018 general elections calls the old state–media relations into question. The new Pakatan Harapan coalition, led by Mahathir Mohamad, has promised freedom for the media. On the other hand, Mahathir's previous stint as prime minister (1981–2003), when he was the BN leader, did not earn him a reputation as a believer in press freedom or civil liberties. At the time of writing it is unclear to what extent his government would grant independence to the government-owned national broadcaster, RTM, or the national news agency, Bernama. RTM still answers to the Ministry of Communications and Multimedia. It operates four television stations and thirty radio stations around the country. Through government financial institutions and statutory bodies, the state also has stakes in private media organisations.

Equally uncertain is how media companies controlled by BN and its cronies will adapt to the new dispensation. Two of the country's main media companies are directly owned by BN parties: UMNO, the alliance's main party, owned the Utusan Malaysia Group, but it relinquished its control in early 2019 when it sold off its half of the shares to a company belonging to a party leader; the Malaysian Chinese Association owns The Star Media Group. Media Prima Berhad – a conglomerate of four television stations, newspapers, radio stations, production houses, and outdoor advertising – was previously aligned to the BN through nominee companies. In 2017, the Japanese investment firm Mitsubishi UFJ became its major shareholder. Astro – a satellite television service that operates more than 160 television channels, radio stations, and internet protocol television (IPTV) – is owned by business tycoon T. Ananda Krishnan, who has benefitted from the Malaysian government's patronage (Gomez, 2018). Krishnan has stakes in Astro and one of the largest telecommunications companies, Maxis, through his entity Usaha Tegas Sdn Bhd, and MEASAT. He also owns other business in the property, oil, and entertainment sectors.

Logging mogul Tiong Hiew King owns the largest Chinese language media in the peninsula through the Media Chinese International Limited. The Lau family, owner of another timber conglomerate, owns the main newspapers in the East Malaysian states of Sabah and Sarawak. The logging and plantation industries in Sabah and Sarawak have mainly benefited from close ties with the regional governments, which enjoyed uncritical domestic media reporting despite international scrutiny on human rights violations. Berjaya Corporation's Vincent Tan, also a known ally of the BN during the Mahathir Mohamad years, owns a free newspaper, *The Sun*, but has held licenses to run pay television, albeit unsuccessfully, and now a satellite television company, Ansa Broadcast.

In Myanmar, the military junta controlled the ownership and regulation of media for six decades and only began relaxing these controls with the appointment of a quasi-civilian government in March 2011, which paved the way for political and media reforms. This opening allowed existing private media to run daily newspapers without prior censorship, and the media in exile to operate in the country. More than thirty media outlets opened in the ethnic states and regions, and they have developed into important sources of information locally (MDIF, 2018). With a GDP per capita half that of Indonesia, however, Myanmar's consumer base and advertising market have not been able to sustain a vibrant commercial media sector. Several newspapers shut down after launching their dailies. Most of the others lack the capacity to engage in high-quality independent journalism.

The broadcast sector is in transition. The government, through the Ministry of Information, and the military own and run television and radio stations. Private broadcasters are dependent on the state infrastructure and have to enter into agreements with the ministry to operate the stations. In April 2017, the government-run MRTV signed two-year contracts with five providers to run digital television channels. The significant change in this arrangement is that unlike the earlier licence holders, who were mainly cronies of the previous military junta, the new joint ventures also include the former media in exile, Mizzima and the Democratic Voice of Burma. But it remains to be seen how much freedom the NLD government will tolerate. The state retains an overall advantage over the private media outlets, given its access to the national coffers, revenue from government and private advertisements, and infrastructure for printing, distribution, and production.

4.3 Disruptions and Continuities

Attempts to counter the trends towards media concentration and state control have been mixed, with independent online media making some breakthroughs. The Internet has provided unprecedented openings for free and independent media as well as political dissenters in Southeast Asian countries with restrictive political environments (Abbott, 2011). But independent online outlets have to contend not only with government restrictions but also with larger competitors that have superior resources (Nain & Venkiteswaran, 2016). Rappler, a Philippine online startup known for its hard-hitting journalism, is one of the latest targets of the Duterte administration's campaign of media harassment and intimidation. It has had to battle trumped-up charges that it has evaded tax and violated rules on foreign ownership and libel.

Although the Internet is still a boon for those on the margins, it has certainly not overturned the advantages enjoyed by more powerful political and business interests (see Section 6). The space has attracted large media organisations and political parties, which have invested significant resources in online platforms to expand their reach and distribution channels. Traditional media, especially in broadcasting, do face competition from new players that are able to use the

Internet to bypass satellite or cable providers. Most of these disrupters, however, are themselves backed by established business corporations. Their business models have included working with the telecommunications giants in Southeast Asia. Examples include companies offering content over the Internet – so-called over-the-top (OTT) media services – such as the Malaysia-based iFlix, which has more than five million online subscribers in 19 markets. In 2017, Malaysia's Media Prima acquired Rev Asia Holdings, a regional digital media group, making it the third largest digital media company in the country after Google and Facebook (Mansor, 2017). In Indonesia, media giants such as the Bakrie Group, MNC, and Trans Corp have been investing heavily in digital platforms, including chat applications, shopping sites, online news, or other e-commerce platforms, to adapt to technological changes and consumer preferences (Tapsell, 2017).

The state and big media corporations dominate the media landscape in a number of countries in Southeast Asia to varying degrees and with different effects. In some cases, the dominance of the large corporations or oligarchs means that media companies can have a strong influence in media policy making. Southeast Asia's media and infocomm regulators, with the possible exception of Thailand before the military coup, do not have a tradition of transparency and independence from the executive branch. Large, establishment media corporations have a seat at the table when policies are being formulated, while potential disrupters and smaller competitors have to lobby frenetically to be heard. In Indonesia, corporate media lobbyists have been known to work with legislators as well as the members of the Indonesian Broadcasting Commission to make the regulatory body take a friendlier approach to the media giants, including by turning a blind eye to media cross-ownership (Dhyatmika, 2014; Masduki, 2017). The pro-government private media in Malaysia, especially the establishment newspapers, were known to be supportive of barriers of entry, including withholding government advertisements for competitors that were seen as being critical of the establishment. In Singapore, there was no open tender when the government decided to allow more competition in media in 2000. It announced as a fait accompli that the state-owned national broadcaster MediaCorp would get a newspaper publishing permit, while the government-friendly Singapore Press Holdings would be allowed to enter the television market. Governments in Southeast Asia have already begun to initiate moves to regulate OTT, partly to monitor content online, and also due to pressure from the dominant media players, which say these platforms should not be exempt from licensing or tax rules (The Edge, 2017; Pornwasin, 2017).

Since people power movements unseated dictators and authoritarian regimes in the Philippines, Thailand, and Indonesia, these countries are often cited as leaders in democratisation in the region. Yet, the gains made should be viewed critically given the illiberal trends described in this and other sections. Myanmar and Malaysia have also sparked great expectations of media liberalisation. Although their media now enjoy more freedom than was thinkable prior to 2010, the two countries have yet to undergo major structural reforms. Meanwhile, the Cambodian government has consolidated its dominance in the July 2018 elections after cracking down on independent media.

Regardless of political system, media ownership patterns in Southeast Asia show oligarchs and cronies playing a prominent role across the region, even as the state – in the form of both civilian governments and the military rule – continues to dominate either directly or indirectly in several countries. The nexus between politics and business results in biased reportage and limits on the range of viewpoints covered, most notably during elections and in the coverage of key policy and economic issues (Houghton & Nain, 2015; Maza, 2018; Nugroho, Putri, & Laksmi, 2012). The proliferation of private media outlets, notably in the broadcast sector, has multiplied viewing choices and satisfied consumers' cravings for entertainment and advertisers' demands for marketing vehicles. But there has been a less-than-proportionate growth in citizens' access to the diverse ideas and opinions they need for democratic self-determination. Broadcast licences, in particular, have gone to political and business elites with little or no appetite for supporting public-interest journalism. Despite the disruptive opportunities presented by digital media, loose controls on cross-media ownership have helped reproduce concentrations of power in the media industries. Non-commercial civic content has been able to squeeze into the regulatory gaps opened up by the Internet, but independent journalism ventures remain vulnerable to both post-publication punishments for dissent as well as formidable commercial competition from corporate media.

5 Media and Intolerance

Until recently, accounts of media and politics tended to equate democratisation with any shift of power from rulers to the people. Observers assumed that any concession the state makes to the popular will would improve human rights. It is now clear, though, that when political space opens up, it may be occupied by popular movements that are anti-democratic, or downright dangerous. In the extreme, state tyranny can be replaced – or augmented – by the tyranny of the majority. Aware of this risk, political theorists have long argued that democratic systems' majoritarian bias must be checked by the vigorous protection of equal rights. The failure to do so is manifest in the wave of intolerant populism that has swept advanced industrial societies in recent years, to the benefit of demagogues and nativist parties.

Southeast Asia is no stranger to eruptions of intolerance and hate. The most extreme of the present-day cases is Myanmar's anti-Rohingya violence, which verges on genocide. In Indonesia, hard-line Muslim groups have mounted hate campaigns against Christians, Chinese, and minority Muslim sects. This section explains such developments and looks at the complex role of the media. Some are victims of intolerance, while others are its instigators. Some are trying to contribute to solutions; others are part of the problem.

Hate speech constitutes a clear ethical abuse of people's right to self-expression. What is less clear is whether and how societies should regulate such breaches. The relationship between free speech and hateful expression is not straightforward. Although hate speech may proliferate when there are no legal limits on permissible speech, it is also true that hate speech tends to cause the greatest harm when freedom of speech is highly restricted. This is because the worst violations of minority rights occur in societies with extreme imbalances of power. In such contexts, the powerful apply speech restrictions in highly discriminatory ways, silencing marginalised communities while permitting dominant groups to engage in hate speech with impunity. Genocides are always preceded by selective silencing, such that target groups are unable to speak out against impending disaster.

International human rights law has grappled with the hate speech problem and emerged with a few key principles. These are enshrined in the International Covenant on Civil and Political Rights (ICCPR), the United Nations' core human rights treaty. The ICCPR's Article 19 protects freedom of expression, while Article 20 requires states to prohibit incitement to hatred, discrimination, or violence. Read together, these provisions draw a distinction between speech that merely offends people's subjective beliefs or feelings, and speech that incites objective harms against vulnerable groups. The former is protected speech under international human rights law, while the latter requires state intervention.

The ASEAN Human Rights Declaration (AHRD), in Article 23, upholds freedom of opinion and expression in terms similar to Article 19 of the ICCPR. Article 22 of the AHRD, like the ICCPR's Article 20, calls for the elimination of discrimination and incitement of hatred, although it only refers to religious intolerance, whereas international human rights law also addresses hatred based on nationality, ethnicity, and other markers of identity. In any case, the AHRD is not a legally binding instrument. The ICCPR is binding on states that have ratified it – six out of ten ASEAN members have done so – but is virtually unenforceable. It carries more moral weight than legal, providing political capital to groups lobbying for human rights.

Thus, it is national laws that hold sway. In Southeast Asian jurisdictions, laws on insult and hate deviate markedly from the ICCPR approach. Across the region, states and non-state actors exploit insult laws to prohibit or punish speech that poses no demonstrable harms to vulnerable groups, but that merely challenges the hegemony of dominant communities and elites. These laws come in different forms, restricting blasphemy, sedition, lèse majesté, or offence against racial and religious feelings. Although worded differently, they share certain problematic features: they are sweeping and subjective, they can be triggered by third-party complaints, and they punish violations with jail terms. As a result, journalists, bloggers, and other citizens regularly feel the sharp end of such laws after expressing views or sharing news that more open societies would consider legitimate contributions to democratic debate.

In Malaysia, for example, the Barisan Nasional government, in power until 2018, investigated journalists under the Sedition Act for merely reporting what establishment figures said about ethnic issues. The country's Internal Security Act, which has since been repealed, was used in 2008 to arrest a reporter from the Chinese-language *Sin Chew Jit Poh* newspaper for reporting the public remarks of a ruling party official to the effect that Chinese were squatters in the country and not deserving of equal rights. Malaysia's Sedition Act remains highly problematic, prohibiting expression that has a tendency to cause ill will – regardless of the real risk of any harmful impact, or the intention of the speaker, or whether the statements are truthful. Although most sedition cases did not result in lengthy detentions or convictions, they contributed to a climate of intimidation, dampening criticism of Malaysia's ethnic discrimination (Lakhdhir, 2015).

Singapore's sedition and internal security legislation is similar to Malaysia's and carries the same risks of overreach. Section 298 of Singapore's Penal Code, copied from colonial-era Indian law, punishes with a jail term of up to three years anyone using any expression found to be deliberately 'wounding the religious or racial feelings of any person'. As in India, the law is usually triggered by members of the public who claim to have been intolerably offended by some provocative expression. In Singapore, the authorities are often able to resolve the matter without resorting to formal charges by persuading the offender to apologise. In one prominent case, however, a teenage blogger was convicted and imprisoned twice. He finally fled to the United States, where he successfully sought political asylum. The boy had posted a vulgar rant against Singaporeans' adulation of the just-deceased Lee Kuan Yew, comparing it to what he considered as mindless devotion to Jesus Christ. He was convicted under Section 298 (George, 2017).

Thailand's unique lèse majesté law (Section 112 of the Criminal Code) belongs in the same category of broad insult laws against which it is extremely difficult for an accused person to defend himself. Like blasphemy, it is a traditional piece of legislation ostensibly enacted to enforce deference towards a supreme moral authority – in Thailand's case, its revered monarchy – but has since become a convenient weapon to brandish against political or ideological opponents. Lèse majesté cases spiked after 2006, not because of any decline in people's veneration for the king, but due to the extreme polarisation that has gripped Thai electoral politics since then, between camps for and against the former billionaire prime minister Thaksin Shinawatra (McCargo, 2017).

When insult laws such as blasphemy are challenged, Southeast Asian states counter that they do not want to follow the example of Western democracies where the denigration of races and religions is allowed. A landmark event in this debate was the 2005 publication of cartoons of the Prophet Mohammed by a Danish newspaper, to challenge what its editors saw as Muslims' unreasonable sensitivity to criticism of their religion. The ensuing riots in 2006 convinced many governments that liberal societies were taking free speech to ridiculous and dangerous limits. Pakistan tabled a draft resolution at the United Nations General Assembly on combating the 'defamation of religions' – the latest round in a campaign by Muslim countries to align international law on freedom of expression with their own taboos against religious offence. The non-binding resolution passed easily, with all ten ASEAN members voting in favour.

Southeast Asian states argue that they need offence laws in order to maintain public order and social harmony. Ironically, though, most of these states have a poor record when it comes to policing the more dangerous problem of incitement to harms – against which international law does require them to intervene. Singapore is perhaps the only Southeast Asian country where the ban on the advocacy of hatred is enforced with equal vigour regardless of which racial or religious communities are involved. Most other governments tend to enforce incitement laws in discriminatory ways, such that disfavoured minority groups receive less protection.

Examples include a headline in the Malay-language *Utusan Malaysia* following the 2013 election. The ruling Malay nationalist party, UMNO, suffered unprecedented losses, raising fears of ethnic riots. In this nervy climate, *Utusan*'s front page banner headline demanded to know, 'Apa lagi Cina mahu?' ('What more do Chinese want?'), instigating Malay readers to blame the result on the Chinese minority's ingratitude. The government took no action against the newspaper for its race-baiting headline. More serious examples of unchecked incitement are found in Myanmar and Indonesia.

5.1 Anti-Muslim Hate in Myanmar

After almost fifty years of military rule, Myanmar's political reforms of 2011, followed by elections in 2015 that were won by Aung San Suu Kyi's National League for Democracy, were heralded as a major advance for democracy in Southeast Asia. Freedom of expression grew dramatically, as noted in Section 2. Exile media such as *Irrawaddy* gave the liberalisation process their vote of confidence by setting up shop in Myanmar. Very quickly, though, the country was mired in ethnic conflict and humanitarian crises. Buddhist–Muslim violence erupted in June 2012. In July 2014, the country's second largest city, Mandalay, experienced two days of riots after unverified rumours circulated that a Muslim tea shop owner had raped a Buddhist worker.

Discrimination against the Rohingya Muslim community of Rakhine State has been particularly extreme. The government does not recognise their identity and nationality: they are referred to as Bengali and treated as illegal immigrants. After some Rohingya turned militant and attacked police and army posts in 2016, government forces stepped up their actions in Rakhine State. They launched a brutal campaign against Rohingya villages in August 2017, which United Nations officials characterised as an ethnic cleansing, if not a full-blown genocide. At least 6,700 Rohingya were killed in the first month of the operation. Some 700,000 Rohingya fled the country (Albert, 2018).

The Rohingya crisis has attracted global attention. Many analysts have pointed fingers at the role of under-regulated social media in circulating hate propaganda. While Facebook is one factor, a full explanation must look deeper at the rise of Burmese-Buddhist majoritarianism in Myanmar's new democracy. Buddhists make up almost nine in ten of Myanmar's population. Anti-Muslim and anti-Indian riots date back to the 1920s and 1930s, occurring alongside uprisings against colonial rule. In anti-Muslim riots of 1938, more than 100 mosques were set on fire; 142 Muslims were killed. The British had allowed free immigration from India; Indians filled colonial government positions and took over huge swathes of agricultural land, causing local resentment. The community of monks, the sangha, were at the forefront of these agitations. They had enjoyed a special status in precolonial times: Buddhism was the kingdom of Burma's state religion for almost a millennium. The king supported the work of the monks, who in turn bestowed legitimacy upon him. By discontinuing this tradition, the British radicalised segments of the sangha (O'Connor, 2017).

The latest round of ethnonationalist hate has again been actively cultivated by radical Buddhist nationalists. The so-called 969 movement surfaced in 2011 and evolved into MaBaTha, the Organization for the Protection of Race and Religion, which was founded in 2013. Hate propaganda by 969 and its infamous monk Wirathu includes hoaxes about Buddhist women being raped or abducted by Muslim men and calls on Buddhists not to patronise Muslim businesses. Hate messages are spread through Facebook, DVDs, pamphlets, and other media.

Although the Constitution prohibits mixing religion and politics, these groups have been able to take advantage of political liberalisation to mobilise Buddhist nationalism, with Muslims demonised as the common foe. The appeal of radical Buddhist nationalists does not hinge mainly on their anti-Muslim agenda; their organisations provide social and cultural services and a sense of belonging to Myanmar people anxious about rapid economic dislocation and insecurity (International Crisis Group, 2017). But the extremists would not have been able to generate the level of violence witnessed, O'Connor (2017) notes, without help from the wider culture, which is already infused with habits of intolerance against Muslims.

The work that goes into potent hate campaigns is always distributed across various actors. There is a division of labour. Individual speech acts may appear innocuous, but the cumulative impact can be deadly. In the Myanmar case, high-profile movement leaders such as Wirathu make hateful comments about Muslims but avoid explicit calls for violence, giving themselves plausible deniability when they are accused of inciting genocide. The most violent language is used by anonymous online commentators and activists on the ground through word of mouth. Government leaders, whose international reputation is at stake, try to appear sober and reasonable. What shocked many observers, though, was the NLD's refusal to condemn unequivocally the extreme violence perpetrated against defenceless Rohingya. Politicians, including Aung San Suu Kyi, framed the crisis as caused by aggression on both sides. The charitable interpretation is that they deem it too politically costly to stand up to a public opinion that was poisoned against Muslims long ago.

Myanmar's media parallel this wider social and political milieu. Hate speech is rampant on Facebook, the dominant platform through which news and information is shared online. Human rights defenders' complaints about the harmful role being played by Facebook in Myanmar received little attention until the company came under pressure for its conduct in the United States and Western Europe. This highlights a structural problem with Facebook's position in the networked Global South. Myanmar's Facebook population of 16 million is sizeable in absolute terms, but their modest per capita income means that they do not amount to a major commercial market. Platforms such as Facebook have little financial incentive to invest in improving the quality of their service there, by hiring enough local-language moderators, for example.

With few exceptions – one being the magazine *Frontier* – domestic media outlets have not been critical of the government's handling of radical Buddhist nationalism and the Rohingya crisis. Brooten (2016) suggests that exile media that benefited from professional training opportunities were generally less susceptible to disinformation and hate campaigns. Yet, *Irrawaddy* – which came in from exile after the 2011 reforms and is one of the country's most internationally celebrated outlets – has toed the government line on the Rohingya issue. It refused to use the Rohingya name and denied their Myanmar nationality. Thus, anti-Muslim rhetoric can be found in mainstream media; it is not just the work of anonymous trolls. Mainstream media have shared dubious images purporting to show Rohingya burning down their own homes. One infamous cartoon by a respected artist depicted the Rohingya as crocodiles swimming away from a bloodied shore, implying that they were in fact the aggressors. The cartoonist showed the crocodiles heading towards sympathetic Western reporters, suggesting that the crisis was the creation of anti-Myanmar media conspiracy. The cartoon covered the entire top half of one newspaper's front page.

The most critical reports and commentaries on Myanmar's anti-Muslim intolerance have come from international media. In 2018, two Myanmarese reporters who had been investigating the murder of Rohingya for the global news agency Reuters were accused of violating secrecy laws and sentenced to seven years' jail. The foreign media's role in monitoring one of the world's most serious humanitarian crises only seems to have stiffened Myanmar nationalism. Standing up to intolerance can invite attack. In 2014, Htin Lin Oo, a former information officer of the NLD, argued in a speech that discriminating against other races or religions was not Buddhist. He pointed out that the Buddha himself was neither a national of Myanmar nor a member of any its main ethnic groups. Extreme nationalism and racism were incompatible with Buddhism, he said. Monks were destroying Buddhism by teaching that loving kindness should be extended only to certain people, he added. Although he was criticising Buddhism's self-styled defenders rather than the religion itself, MaBaTha monks successfully agitated for his conviction under Myanmar's blasphemy law, for which he was sentenced to two years' hard labour.

5.2 Hard-Line Muslim Intolerance in Indonesia

Similar dynamics have afflicted Indonesia. After the fall of the authoritarian Suharto regime in 1998, Indonesia democratised rapidly. Like in Myanmar, though, democratic values such as reciprocity and civility did not completely fill the space opened up by the state's retreat. Rising intolerance has proved to be a major problem. Although international attention tends to focus on the occasional explosion of jihadist terror, simmering religious intolerance has arguably had a wider impact. Its exploitation by political actors affects election outcomes, distracts from major problems such as corruption, and prevents minority communities from enjoying equal rights.

Indonesia is home to more Muslims than any other country; they make up around 87 per cent of its population. Islam is not the country's official religion. The national ideology of Pancasila upholds belief in one god, but official recognition is extended to the world's other major faiths alongside Islam. The secular aspects of Indonesian democracy have always been contested by religious nationalists. Post-Suharto democratisation gave hard-line Islamist groups more space to push their exclusivist worldviews. They are diverse in their ideological underpinnings and their methods. For example, Hizbut Tahrir Indonesia (HTI, Indonesia Party of Liberation) is part of an international movement promoting a worldwide caliphate; it was banned in 2017 but remains influential among the educated middle class. Another prominent player, Front Pembela Islam (FPI, the Islamic Defenders Front), is a thuggish network that was covertly marshalled by the army to counter anti-government protestors soon after Suharto's resignation. It has since taken on a life of its own, instigating moral panics and marketing its services as an enforcer of morality. There are also several Muslim-based political parties, an influential Majelis Ulama Indonesia (the clerical body), and a religious affairs ministry that has not had a strong record in protecting religious equality.

Compared with Myanmar, Indonesia's tendencies towards intolerance are more fiercely resisted (Kunkler, 2013). The influential Christian minority and the predominantly Hindu province of Bali are among the buffers protecting Indonesian democracy's secular pillars. Within Indonesian Islam, a robust civil society opposes the exclusivist Islamist worldview. The country's two largest Muslim organisations, Nahdlatul Ulama and Muhammadiyah, oppose violence and have moderated the impact of hard-line groups. The largest political parties are secular. The effects of this engagement, however, have been two-way. While they have stopped the Islamists from taking over Indonesia, many moderates and secularists have in the process internalised some of the rhetoric and agenda of the religious groups, resulting in a mainstreaming of values and discourses that were once on the fringe (Van Bruinessen, 2011).

Religious and ethnic identity is a potent resource for political contenders. Since groups tend to be most cohesive when facing a common enemy, the most unscrupulous exponents of identity politics orchestrate hatred against vulnerable minorities. Victims have included Christian congregations whose plans to build churches have been obstructed by Muslim group activists. Minorities within the Muslim community, particularly the Ahmadiya sect and Shia Muslims, have suffered discrimination and violent attacks by extreme Sunni groups. More recently, some hard-line Muslim groups have resuscitated the communist bogey as a cover for attacking liberals and secularists.

Indonesia's plural media landscape reflects the full range of perspectives, from the tolerant to the hateful. Social media circulates disinformation and hate speech. In 2018, authorities tried to eliminate the Muslim Cyber Army (MCA), an amorphous and extensive network. MCA's repertoire included a viral video that encouraged viewers to report individuals perceived to have insulted Islam or religious leaders. Until it was taken down by Facebook, it had a page publicising a list of such 'wanted' individuals along with their addresses and contact details. This was usually enough to instigate vigilante action within a few days. The mobs intimidated victims into issuing apologies, or handed them to the police for allegedly violating the blasphemy law. In some cases, the offensive content was itself fabricated by MCA and shared through imposter Facebook and Twitter accounts. A high proportion of targets are critics of FPI and its leader, as well as supporters of the Joko Widodo government, suggesting that MCA activists are more political hitmen than morality police (Juniarto, 2018).

Intolerance is not bred only by clandestine groups such as MCA. High-profile celebrity preachers such as Felix Siauw, who is associated with HTI, have helped to mainstream exclusionary worldviews that challenge Pancasila. Siauw has mastered the full suite of outreach modalities. In addition to having four million Facebook followers, he authors and publishes books, speaks at mosques, and runs meetups for youths (Hew, 2018). As for Indonesian television, it offers a steady stream of religious programming, the stars of which are charismatic preachers not known for nuance in their interpretation of Islamic teaching. Muslim soap operas, similarly, have plots that promote binary thinking, with outwardly pious Muslims always shown in a positive light (Hamid, 2018).

Professional journalism in Indonesia is much more developed than in Myanmar. Unlike the Burmese junta, which exercised strict prepublication censorship, Suharto's New Order regime allowed enough pluralism for journalists to develop their professional ethos and capacity, even if they could not always express it (Steele, 2005). Therefore, when Indonesia finally democratised, media organisations such as the *Kompas* newspaper, *Tempo* magazine, and the Alliance of Independent Journalists (AJI) were able to rise to the occasion. They have tried to promote democratic values and resist the rising tide of intolerance. AJI – together with the Press Council (Dewan Pers) and newer civil society organisations such as Masyarakat Anti Fitnah Indonesia (Mafindo, the anti-hoax community network) – conduct training to help media workers and consumers deal with hate speech. Workshops for journalists in Maluku have helped to turn the media there from provocateurs of Christian–Muslim riots to peacebuilders (Lowry & Littlejohn, 2006).

Indonesia's more liberal media and civil society organisations are generally careful not to rile the conservative Muslim ground, especially because hard-line groups like FPI are on a perpetual witch-hunt. Unless they are willing to endure harassment and intimidation, including charges of blasphemy, adherents to what Indonesians term 'Islam Liberal' must bite their tongue when they see their religion hijacked by self-proclaimed defenders of the faith for clearly political or material gain. Indonesia's de facto national newspaper, *Kompas*, is in a particularly awkward position. Its 'original sin' of having been founded by Catholic Indonesians makes it especially vulnerable to the charge of being anti-Muslim (Wijayanto, 2017).

The destructive power of religious identity was on full display in the campaign to dislodge the governor of Jakarta, Basuki Tjahaja Purnama, popularly known as Ahok. An ethnic Chinese Christian, he had been the target of vicious identity politics the moment he entered politics. At first, it appeared that his reputation as an effective, problem-solving administrator would protect him. Indeed, so confident was he in Jakarta residents' pragmatic attitude that he took on FPI publicly, arguing for a ban on the hard-line group. Then, in 2016, the outspoken governor told a gathering of his constituents to go ahead and vote against him if they believed his opponents' lies that the Quran forbids Muslims from electing non-Muslims. His enemies latched onto the throwaway remark. They claimed he had said that the Quran itself was deceiving the people. A video of the speech with crucial words omitted from the subtitles appeared online with a provocative caption. FPI and other hard-line groups mobilised major demonstrations and instigated blasphemy charges. Basuki's political allies (including president Joko Widodo) and media with no love for the hardliners (such as *Kompas*) had to tread gingerly around the controversy instead of calling out what was clearly a cynical and deceptive use of religion for political goals. Basuki not only lost the election in April 2017 but also was sentenced to two years' jail for blasphemy.

5.3 Dark Side of People Power

Compared to twentieth-century atrocities – Cambodia's Khmer Rouge in 1975–79, and Indonesia's anti-communist purge in 1965–66 – Southeast

Asia's twenty-first-century descents into mass violence have been smaller in scale. What is remarkable about today's bigotry is that it is taking place in relatively open societies with independent domestic media and ample foreign media scrutiny. It appears to belong to the 'post-truth' era, in which publics resist available facts and choose to believe what conforms with their strongly held worldviews. It depends less on the totalitarian-style concealment of human rights abuses and more on the cognitive biases of extremely polarised societies. Often, abuses occur in plain sight but are denied, diminished, or rationalised away by dominant groups.

One explanation for this polarisation is Huntington's (1996) highly evocative 'clash of civilisations' thesis that, with the end of the ideologically driven Cold War, global conflict would occur mainly along ethno-religious lines. Although this theory has been largely discredited among scholars of politics, there remains a strong tendency among observers to frame conflicts as rooted in irreconcilable cultural differences and the visceral pull of ethno-religious identities. However, the more sociologically sound interpretation – which is usually echoed by human rights workers on the ground – is that tensions are mostly due to economic instability and insecurity. Exploiting people's anxiety, political entrepreneurs accentuate and sharpen racial and religious identities in order to mobilise collective action. Eruptions of intolerance and hate in Southeast Asia, therefore, are not spontaneous combustions caused by the interaction of diverse communities answering to higher callings; they are engineered by elite actors for political and economic gain (George, 2016).

Hate propaganda plays a key role in these events, suggesting that speech regulation should be central to any policy response. For reasons already mentioned above, using the law has tended to backfire. Instead of rewarding tolerance, offence laws encourage extreme groups to display rowdy indignation at expression they do not like. The convictions of Htin Lin Oo in Myanmar and Ahok in Indonesia were clear cases of blasphemy law being weaponised against hardliners' opponents. Incitement laws, meanwhile, do not serve their legitimate purpose when enforced in a selective manner, as tends to be the case when they are not underpinned by a firm commitment to equality.

Rallying cries that threaten others' equal rights have been alarmingly effective in Southeast Asia. It is expressed as religious nationalism in Myanmar and Indonesia, and xenophobia in Cambodia (anti-Vietnamese) and Vietnam (anti-Chinese), for example. In the Philippines, home of the original 'People Power' revolution, the authoritarian populist Rodrigo Duterte initiated an extrajudicial killing spree claiming some 20,000 lives, with little cost to his popularity. The pattern corresponds with survey evidence (Shin, 2015) that Southeast Asians' support for democracy is shallow. While the vast majority of people want to choose their leaders, their understanding of democracy may be neither liberal nor inclusive. They may instead favour more paternalistic leadership, and a relationship with power that is more clientelist than rights-based. While more research is needed to establish if this is indeed the case, what is already clear is that the region's civic ethos is dangerously weak.

6 Digital Media Disruptions

It is May 2018, and Malaysia is in the midst of a gripping general election campaign. Mahathir Mohamad, chairman of the Pakatan Harapan opposition coalition, is on stage addressing an open-air rally, or ceramah, in a large field next to a majestic mosque in Putrajaya. The ninety-two-year-old politician is demonstrating his effortless mastery of the ancient political skill of orating to a public assembly. Some 10,000 people have waited till past 11 pm to listen to a living legend, reaffirming the continued relevance of this most traditional form of electioneering in contemporary Malaysia.

But the ceramah has changed over the decades. Not just a venue for direct, face-to-face communication, it has also become a media event, a performance staged for print and broadcast news outlets. And now, in 2018, it is simultaneously a social media phenomenon. Audience members regularly turn to their smartphones to share photos, videos, and comments. On cue, they wave their glowing phones overhead in concert to create a vivid memory – and an Instagrammable moment. At the end of the night, Mahathir himself holds his phone up to the crowd, presumably to capture the scene for his @chedetofficial Twitter feed. The rally, like almost all opposition events, would receive no coverage in most mainstream newspapers the next morning. But opposition politicians were accustomed to this and had two decades of experience in using the Internet to bypass mainstream media gatekeepers. Mahathir himself had been a fast learner after quitting the ruling party and thus losing the privileges of establishment media access. He and his Pakatan colleagues could rely on its own online platforms as well as independent news sites such as *Malaysiakini* to get their message out. They would go on to win the election, ousting Southeast Asia's longest-lasting elected regime.

This final section examines the role the Internet plays in the region's political landscape. It is a technology of extraordinary, transformative power. But precisely because it has changed so many things so palpably and in such a short time, it has been difficult to come to grips with it. The tendency to underestimate its potential is matched only by the opposite risk, of exaggerating its impact. Ever since the Internet became available to the general public in the 1990s, analysts have been trying to understand just how revolutionary this undeniably disruptive technology would be. The Internet is much less amenable to censorship than earlier communication technologies. Furthermore, its architecture gives users at the edges of the network the power to create and roll out whole new functions – from web browsing, to blogging, to video sharing, to social media, and so on – making it an endlessly 'generative' technology (Zittrain, 2008). Technology buffs are not coy about proclaiming the liberating power of the Internet, and this has become an irresistible narrative frame for news media reporting on political conflict and change. The Arab Spring of 2010–11, most famously, was widely attributed to social media.

The scholarly work on this subject has been more circumspect, pointing out that the Internet has been neither a necessary nor a sufficient factor for democratisation. The technology has certainly opened up new opportunities for political actors, but exactly who makes use of those openings, and how, is not preordained. As noted in our opening section, political space can be contested in complex and sometimes contradictory ways. This section is written in that vein, taking stock of the Internet's impact on two of the region's most resilient regimes (at least up till early 2018) – Vietnam and Malaysia. At the risk of oversimplification, we identify three periods in the Internet's brief history. First, there was an initial period during which insurgents had the upper hand, and regulators were undecided about whether and how to catch up. This was followed by, second, more determined action by governments to repress what was becoming a threat they could no longer ignore. In the current third phase, coercion continues, but governments and ruling parties are also major players in their own right, colonising online space so effectively that the Internet is now a threat to dissidents and marginalised groups as well as an opportunity. It is an arena where powerful interests mobilize attacks on their opponents and where cyber armies flood the public with disinformation and propaganda.

6.1 Vietnam's Selective Embrace of the Internet

The Communist Party of Vietnam (CPV), like its Chinese big brother, has tried to embrace the free market while keeping much of the economy in its own hands and maintaining its firm grip on politics. Acknowledging that the Internet had become essential infrastructure for economic activity, the government liberalised online access in the late 2000s. State-owned Vietnam Post and Telecommunications Corporation and military-owned Viettel, which together control around 80 per cent of the internet access market, have been major players in getting people online.

More than one-third of the population was using the Internet by 2012. Smartphone penetration reached nearly 30 per cent in 2017 (Freedom House,

2018b). Blogs were at first the online medium of choice but were quickly overtaken by social networks. Facebook, with more than 50 million active accounts in 2017, is perhaps the country's most important and influential channel for information (Bui, 2018). The platform has become so indispensable for small businesses and advertisers that the government cannot shut it down without hurting the economy. Facebook has an agenda-setting role. Most mainstream journalists have active Facebook accounts and pick up story ideas and viewpoints from the posts they read.

'[S]ocial media and the blogosphere have become the major battlegrounds in Vietnam for contesting ideas about and norms of governance and discourses on the political regime', says Bui (2018: 100). The rapacious conduct of corrupt officials and big businesses frequently results in flagrant injustices at the grassroots. When suppressed by state media, people's grievances have found a ready outlet through independent blogs and social media, or what Vietnamese call 'left side press' (*bao le trai*). Most of the bloggers live in Vietnam. They pick up issues that are avoided by mainstream media, touching on human rights, economic justice, and relations with China (Duong, 2017). There are also many anonymous blogs, such as *Quan Lam Bao* (Officials Doing Journalism), which was prominent in 2012 for attacking then-premier Nguyen Tan Dung. 'With the use of social media, civil society actors can push the boundaries of what is acceptable to the state and claim an expanding political space', says Bui (2018: 109).

Controversies in which the Internet played an important role included a 2009 debate over bauxite mining. Critics argued that a major project in the Central Highlands would displace poor minorities, cause environmental damage, and give Chinese partners too much economic influence. Three intellectuals drafted a petition, which developed into a blog, *Bauxite Vietnam*, as a hub for this debate. The blog evolved into a generic site dealing with various sensitive political issues.

One successful Internet-enabled civil society campaign was a movement to save 6,700 trees from felling in Hanoi in 2015. The central government intervened and reversed the city officials' plans, even disciplining some of them. Another major episode was a 2016 environmental disaster linked to pollution from a Taiwanese steel factory. It decimated the fishing and tourism industries in Vietnam's central provinces, destroying the livelihoods of hundreds of thousands of people. Evidence of a crisis was plain to see, as millions of dead fish washed up along the central coast. Street protests erupted in the main cities. Mainstream media did not cover the demonstrations, channeling discontent online. In 2017, Facebook enabled Vietnamese activists and ordinary citizens to share news and opinions about a hostage drama arising from a land dispute.

Villagers held police and government officials for more than a week to protect their land from appropriation. Although the authorities insisted that the land belongs to the military, they neither punished the villagers nor proceeded with development plans – probably because of the spotlight of embarrassing publicity provided by social media.

The government's blocking and filtering system is not as elaborate as China's. Internet service providers implement censorship of blacklisted websites. These tend to be popular local and overseas-based political blogs and sites on human rights, democracy, and other themes frowned on by the party. Other sensitive issues include border and maritime disputes with China, and any criticism of the party's top leaders. Access to the Vietnamese language sites of external broadcasters such as the American-funded Radio Free Asia and the BBC tends to be intermittent. During periods of localised unrest, such as the April 2017 hostage incident, the authorities have been known to restrict the mobile data signal and even mobile telephony. As street protests were mobilised over the 2016 environmental disaster case, Facebook and Instagram were blocked temporarily, though many users were able to turn to circumventing tools. Like in China, censorship is partly outsourced to internet intermediaries such as internet service providers and cybercafé owners.

Post-publication punishments include fines and lengthy jail terms. To facilitate enforcement, Vietnamese companies operating blogging platforms and social networks are required to locate servers within the country and store posts for ninety days. Internet users are subject to fines by administrative fiat if they post content critical of the government, party, or national heroes. Such coercion occasionally backfires on the state. In 2015, authorities fined a teacher VND 5 million (US $220) for a Facebook post describing a provincial chief as arrogant. Two others were fined for liking and sharing the post. These actions provoked such unhappiness that the fines were eventually withdrawn.

There has been no relaxation, however, in the tough policy against dissent. The alternative blogs *Que Choa* and *Anh Ba Sam* came to a halt in 2014 when their owners were detained. After human rights activists set up Luong Tam (Conscience) TV as a YouTube channel in 2015, employees were harassed and detained. In 2017, a prominent blogger, Nguyen Ngoc Nhu Quynh – who had reported on the coastal pollution disaster and co-founded a network of bloggers – was sentenced to ten years' jail. In 2018, three democracy activists were sent to jail for four to eight years for posting seventeen video clips deemed to be spreading propaganda against the state; seven bloggers were handed prison terms averaging more than ten years. The government's unabated tendency to mete out extreme punishments for speech crimes places Vietnam among the least free countries in Asia.

The government has also used economic sticks. It has been able to pressure foreign companies' Vietnam units to stop advertising on Facebook and YouTube. It has also pushed Vietnamese companies to withdraw advertising alongside critical articles. Individuals too face economic punishment. In 2013, journalist Nguyen Dac Kien lost his newspaper job after he posted a blog criticising the speech of party general secretary Nguyen Phu Trong.

The government does not confine itself to a reactionary mode. It has taken proactive steps to shape online public opinion and defend leaders against criticism. Praising Facebook as a communication tool, the government started launching official Facebook pages in 2015. It also engages in more covert operations. Known pro-party bloggers include retired officials, researchers, soldiers, and mainstream media journalists. It is generally assumed that the party pays them as part of a network of hundreds of writers employed by the propaganda department to spread the party line on specially created websites and on existing forums. 'On the one hand, the CPV refuses to recognize blogs as a journalistic activity and continues to crackdown on activist bloggers. On the other hand, blogs have been used by government officials to influence public opinion, expose political scandals and publicize sensationalist news', says Duong (2017: 385).

In addition to online messages centrally coordinated by the propaganda department, there are also bloggers paid by individual leaders and factions and departments at various levels of the state. Some of these blogs leak scandalous information, usually in the run-up to major political events, suggesting that they are being used by factions jostling for power within the establishment. One such blog, *Chan Dung Quyen Luc* (Portrait of Power), carried corruption accusations against senior leaders in the two months leading up to party central committee plenum in January 2015. The site did not target the prime minister, who defended social media around that time as a necessity for Vietnam. The bloggers behind the site were never exposed or punished, adding credence to the theory that the blog was set up to target the prime minister's rivals (Duong, 2017; Bui, 2018).

Such examples show that dynamics of liberalisation and censorship in Vietnam are not straightforward. The regime, or elements within it, may be motivated to allow debates to flow, or not. Its decisions are not dictated by policy positions or ideological commitments as much as shaped by political interests that are highly contextual. In 2018, for example, major newspapers suddenly broke their silence about the 1988 Johnson South Reef Skirmish between the Vietnamese and Chinese navies. For years, citizens had been confined to Facebook when they wanted to remember the fallen soldiers and draw parallels with current territorial disputes in the South China Sea. Suddenly, the authorities decided that it was time to allow some airing of nationalist sentiment through mainstream media, albeit minus any discussion of contemporary disputes.

Pushback against censorship does not only occur in online media. In 2012, a fish farmer and his family used firearms against policemen and soldiers trying to evict them a year before the end of his lease. A month later, two newspapers ran reports critical of the local officials behind the eviction. The party leadership not only allowed but even praised this rare instance of exposé journalism. The leadership probably saw that the scandal was too big to sweep under the rug. Moreover, by framing it as a singular and localised breach by rogue officials rather than a symptom of the endemic corruption reaching the very top of the Politburo, such media coverage 'protected the party's proclaimed status as the benevolent parent of national development' with the 'popular mandate to address the grievances of the people while reasserting its control on the periphery' (Cain, 2014: 87). This was an instance of the selective liberalisation described in Section 3.

6.2 Malaysia's Brittle No Censorship Guarantee

The largest component of Malaysia's new governing coalition, Parti Keadilan Rakyat, has long been committed to democratisation. So has another key coalition partner, the Democratic Action Party. At the time of writing, there is a realistic prospect of substantial media reforms (see Section 2). Just how deep these will go, however, is too early to tell. This section focuses, therefore, on the media system under the ousted Barisan Nasional (BN) regime, which had dominated the country's politics from independence in 1957. An account of that system is of more than merely historical interest. Pre-2018 structures and norms are likely to linger to some extent. While the election result was widely characterised as a 'tsunami', there was little expectation of a transition of the magnitude experienced by Indonesia in 1998 or Myanmar post-2011. Besides, understanding the first two decades of the country's experience with the Internet has theoretical value beyond Malaysia, helping shed light on the relationship between online media, traditional media, and other actors in political space.

Like in Vietnam, the public Internet arrived in Malaysia at a time when politics was dominated by an authoritarian regime with no desire to loosen its grip on news media. There was a major difference in the degree of control, of course. Malaysia in the 1990s already had competitive multiparty elections. The mainstream media, although subject to discretionary licensing, was not entirely owned and operated by the state. The Malaysian government, however, faced essentially the same dilemma as their Vietnamese counterparts: whether to allow onto its territory a radically new medium that would challenge its control of public discourse. Like Vietnam, Malaysia's affirmative answer was compelled by economic motivations. The anticipated cost of abstinence was too high, given how quickly the Internet was becoming essential infrastructure for economic activity. So anxious was the Malaysian government to show high-tech investors that it was in tune with the digital age that it even issued a no-censorship guarantee in 1996 for its vaunted Multimedia Super Corridor investment zone. In this regard, it was one step ahead of rival Singapore, which could only commit itself to 'light touch' internet regulation.

Malaysia's first generation of bloggers, such as Raja Petra Kamaruddin, appeared on time to contribute to the Reformasi protest movement of 1998, sparked by the arrest of the popular politician Anwar Ibrahim and resulted in the formation of Keadilan, which would gain power twenty years later. Keadilan and other opposition parties were quick to develop a presence on the web, and later social media. When the Islamic party PAS was ordered to cut the frequency of its print newspaper from biweekly to bimonthly in 2000, it responded by boosting its daily online version, *Harakah Daily*. It introduced online videos as early as 2001. The journalist-owned news site *Malaysiakini* was also launched around the same period, growing to become the region's most successful venture in independent online political news (George, 2006).

One test of the Internet's democratising potential is whether individual online expression – which may amount to little more than 'slacktivism' – can develop into offline collective action. Malaysia is not short of examples of Internet-assisted social mobilisation. Bersih, or the Coalition for Clean and Fair Elections, showcased how the Internet could be leveraged by committed civil society actors to mobilise mass offline support. With roots in a joint action committee of opposition party leaders, the first Bersih rally was a mass walk in 2007. In 2011, Bersih 2.0 organised a demonstration of more than 10,000 people, using mainly Facebook and Twitter. In 2012, an estimated 80,000–100,000 turned up for Bersih 3.0, making it Malaysia's largest protest event since independence (Abbott, 2013). Beyond calling Malaysians out to the streets and providing real-time hyperlocal intelligence on how to avoid riot police, Bersih's social media activism also helped build 'a sense of (pan-racial, pan-religious) collective identity and community' (Weiss, 2014: 100).

Blogging also provided individuals a new route toward political candidacy, bypassing the traditional avenues of serving at party branches or community organisations. Tony Pua and Jeff Ooi, for example, were recruited by the opposition Democratic Action Party and successfully fielded in the 2008 elections after having established themselves as opinion leaders through their blogs.

Gong (2011) found that in the 2008 election, candidates with blogs had higher chances of winning elections than non-bloggers.

Malaysia's 1996 no-censorship promise meant only that the government would neither engage in blocking and filtering of online content nor require content providers to be licensed. It did not protect online speech from the customary panoply of post-publication punishments, such as defamation and sedition. In 2003, for example, police raided *Malaysiakini*'s newsroom and confiscated its computers as part of a sedition probe into a reader's letter published on the site. Like Singapore's 'calibrated coercion' (Section 3), whatever self-restraint the Malaysian government showed in censoring the Internet was not due to any attachment to liberal values. Its actions were guided more by an instrumental cost-benefit analysis, the results of which would vary as ground realities changed. Thus, as online dissent became more powerful, the government's tolerance wore thin. In the March 2008 general election, the opposition made unprecedented gains, prompting Prime Minister Abdullah Badawi to declare that the ruling party may have underestimated the Internet. Although this may have just been a convenient excuse for his government's poor showing – it is unlikely that the Internet was the decisive factor – the authorities did ratchet up repression soon after. Later the same year, they used the Internal Security Act against blogger Raja Petra Kamaruddin. They also blocked his blog, *Malaysia Today*, effectively abandoning their no-censorship guarantee.

When Prime Minister Najib Razak (2009–18) was besieged by a gargantuan corruption scandal surrounding a state investment fund, 1MDB, government repression grew increasingly heavy-handed and arbitrary. The Internet was not immune. In 2015, the government blocked Bersih's website in the run-up to street protests demanding Najib's resignation. It also blocked *Sarawak Report*, a blog that played a leading role in exposing the 1MDB affair. The blogging platform Medium was also blocked for refusing to take down a *Sarawak Report* article. *The Malaysian Insider*, a popular news site, was blocked by authorities in 2016 after it published a controversial 1MDB article.

Another major development after 2008 was the entry of government and ruling party actors as powerful online players in their own right. In its first decade, the Malaysian online public sphere was dominated by oppositional voices. The government resorted to punishment and deterrence of online dissent and fell back on its hegemony over offline political space. Post-2008, however, the government became more proactive, investing substantially in its own online propaganda capacity and attempting to flood cyberspace with its own messages. In addition to getting all ministers on social media, tactics included organising volunteers and paid commentators to post comments, and creating fake Twitter and Facebook accounts to magnify perceived support. By the 2013 general election, several pro-government bloggers were playing an active role. UMNO created a new media unit with more than 200 full-time and part-time workers (Tapsell, 2018). Western public relations firms earned millions of dollars by assisting Najib's media campaigns (Tapsell, 2013). Opposition parties employ similar tactics, with the real losers being citizens in search of fair and independent information and analysis. 'As political parties in Malaysia are becoming increasingly involved in cyberspace, the medium is becoming a place of manipulated content facilitated by political staff, public-relations experts, paid bloggers and "cybertroopers",' Tapsell observed in 2013 (p. 48).

Thus, the Internet was never a risk-free environment for dissenters and was increasingly populated by pro-establishment actors. Nevertheless, it was no small matter that Malaysians could now own and operate a mass medium without prior permission from the authorities – and at a small fraction of the cost required to run print or broadcast outlets. Digital media made it easier for political and civil society activists to mobilise and organise dissent and for ordinary citizens to share news and opinions. All this amounted to a radical expansion of political space.

What is more debatable is whether the Internet played a decisive role in the toppling of BN in 2018. Ten years earlier, some reviews of the 2008 general election – including by the then-premier, as mentioned earlier – cited the Internet as a major factor behind the ruling party's losses. The next polls, in 2013, were dubbed a social media election on account of the unprecedented efforts by all major political parties in that space. In 2018, cyberspace was undoubtedly a major battleground alongside offline space. Indeed, it was so much a part of the elections that it was hard to conceive of it as a separate sphere. Over the years, internet technologies have penetrated practically every part of political life, including traditional activities such as ceramah, as described in the introduction to this section. There are numerous other examples: Mahathir's emotive 2018 campaign videos, with the production values of a slick television commercial but distributed through YouTube; or political cartoonist Zunar's hand-drawn attacks on Najib, converted into animated memes for Twitter and WhatsApp. The boundaries between online and offline worlds are harder to distinguish – and it is perhaps getting irrelevant to try to do so.

For more than two decades, journalists covering elections and contentious politics around the world have been drawn to the role of the Internet as a stock story angle. But in Malaysia by 2018, there was little that seemed novel about the Internet. Instead, the spotlight was on the re-entry of former Prime Minister Mahathir into electoral politics. This – together with the outrage over Najib's unbridled kleptocracy – was the real game-changer, uniting a fractured opposition and winning over sufficient Malay voters from the ruling party.

6.3 The Future of Media and Politics in Southeast Asia

In Vietnam and Malaysia, as well as in other parts of the region, governments allowed and facilitated internet use because of the technology's economic promise. This entailed a political trade-off, even if the incompatibility between new media and authoritarian politics may have been overstated. Since around 2010, it has become clearer that the two can coexist. The political space opened up by the Internet is not the preserve of pro-democratic forces (Morozov, 2012). On the contrary, groups with superior offline resources – which in politically centralised regimes invariably include the state – are able to parlay that advantage online. Today, the main research gap concerning the Internet and politics is no longer how groups on the margins use new technologies to contest the power centre, but how the centre – usually aided by major platform companies and private consultants – has built up its capacity to colonise the contested digital space. Overall, the internet disruption has pluralised media and communication without flattening power differentials.

This underscores a point made in Section 1 about the limitations of 'container thinking' in media studies, which has favoured categorising media systems according to their broad national characteristics – 'authoritarian', 'free', and so on. This habit tends to essentialise national media systems, neglecting their internal diversity. It also focuses on readily observable changes to political institutions and systems – regime changes and legal reforms, in particular – while overlooking subtler and more complex shifts in how power flows through the media system, and how opportunities for participation can both broaden and narrow at the same time.

The main thread running through this study of media and politics in Southeast Asia is that powerful actors' means of control and repression, old and new, can work in concert with, or parallel to, trends towards commercialisation, the growth of identity-based politics, and the spread of digital technologies. In Section 1, we also pointed out that the media-and-power question is further complicated by the fact that democratisation could refer to several different things. From what we have observed, it is clear that trends in Southeast Asia can be interpreted in multiple ways, depending on what we mean by democratisation:

1. Democratisation as regime change. Media contributed to Indonesia's Reformasi and the end of Suharto's New Order regime, but also to the hegemonic domination of Singapore's People's Action Party.

2. Democratisation as a change in governance style. The Internet has helped to amplify ground voices and dissenting views, nudging most states, even communist Vietnam, to show some openness and responsiveness to the popular will.
3. Democratisation as greater public access to information and ideas. Commercial media have in theory broken the government's monopoly in most countries, but in practice may fail to serve citizens' needs, often because they are themselves organs of their owners' political and business interests.
4. Democratisation as wider and deeper citizen participation. In practically all Southeast Asian countries, the Internet has given more groups a voice and enabled citizens to mobilise and engage with power more effectively.
5. Democratisation as normative change. The media should cultivate the democratic values in favour of liberty, equality, and respect for difference. Arguably, no country's media have done well on this score. Indeed, the media may have contributed to political polarisation in Thailand and the Philippines, and hate propaganda in Myanmar.

Trends in Southeast Asian media and power will continue to present more contradictions than convergence. It is safe to say that technology, the theme of this section, will remain a key driver of change. So will competing visions of nationhood, expressed through various forms of identity politics that challenge inclusive constitutions. The tension between journalism's commercial impulses and its democratic role will generate both cynical exploitation of media power by corporate interests, as well as inspiring examples of public service journalism holding the powerful to account.

Political change – and resistance to change – should remain a compelling focus for scholarship, not least because Southeast Asian nations' trajectories have been so difficult to foresee. The opening up of Myanmar and Malaysia took most analysts by surprise, as did the Philippines' authoritarian turn. In 2010, it would have sounded outlandish to predict that, in 2018, Nobel Peace Prize laureate Aung San Suu Kyi would be named an Oppressor of the Press by the Committee to Protect Journalists; or that Malaysia's pro-democracy movement would be counting on its old nemesis Mahathir Mohammed to fulfil their dreams of media reform. If the changes over the last decade tell us anything, it is that making predictions about this vibrant and variegated corner of Asia would be foolhardy.

Bibliography

Abbott, J. (2013). Introduction: Assessing the Social and Political Impact of the Internet and New Social Media in Asia. *Journal of Contemporary Asia* 43(4), 579–90. doi:https://doi.org/10.1080/00472336.2013.785698.

Abbott, Jason P. (2011). Cacophony or Empowerment? Analysing the Impact of New Information Communication Technologies and New Social Media in Southeast Asia. *Journal of Current Southeast Asian Affairs* 30(4), 3–31.

Albert, E. (2018). *The Rohingya Crisis*. New York, NY: Council on Foreign Relations. www.cfr.org/backgrounder/rohingya-crisis

Arendt, H. (1970). *On Violence*. Orlando, FL: Harcourt Brace Jovanovich.

Bagidikian, B. (2004). *The New Media Monopoly*. Beacon Press.

Besley, T. and Prat, A. (2006). Handcuffs for the Grabbing Hand? Media Capture and Government Accountability. *The American Economic Review*, 96(3), 720–36.

Bonura, C. (2015). *Political Polarization, Transition, and Civil Society in Thailand and Malaysia*. Washington, DC: Middle East Institute. www.mei.edu/content/map/political-polarization-transition-and-civil-society-thailand-and-malaysia (accessed 20 July 2018)

Brooten, L. (2016). Burmese Media in Transition. *International Journal of Communication* 10, 182–99.

Bui, H. T. (2018). The new meaning of political participation in cyberspace: social media and collective action in Vietnam's authoritarianism. In Hansson, E. and Weiss, M. L. (eds.). *Political Participation in Asia: Defining and Deploying Political Space*. London: Routledge, pp. 112–29.

Cain, G. (2014). Kill One to Warn One Hundred: the Politics of Press Censorship in Vietnam. *The International Journal of Press/Politics* 19(1), 85–107. doi:https://doi.org/10.1177/1940161213508814.

Cambodian Centre for Independent Media and Reporters Without Borders. (2017). Media Ownership Monitor: Cambodia. http://cambodia.mom-rsf.org (accessed 2 October 2018)

Campbell, C. (2017). *World Press Trends 2017. Frankfurt, Germany: WAN-IFRA*. anp.cl/wp-content/uploads/2017/10/WAN-IFRA_WPT_2017.pdf

Carpentier, N. (2011). The Concept of Participation. If They Have Access and Interact, Do They Really Participate? *CM Communication Management Quarterly*, 6(21), 13–36.

Cornwall, A. and Goetz, A. M. (2005). Democratizing Democracy: Feminist Perspectives. *Democratization*, *12*(5), 783–800. doi.org/10.1080/135103405 00322181

Couldry, N. and Hepp, A. (2012). Comparing media cultures. In Esser, F. and Hanitzsch, T. (eds.). *The Handbook of Comparative Communication Research*. New York: Routledge, pp. 249–61.

Dhakidae, D. (1991). *The State, the Rise of Capital and the Fall of Political Journalism: Political Economy of Indonesian News Industry*. PhD Dissertation, Cornell University.

Dhyatmika, W. (2014). Who Owns the News in Indonesia? *Nieman Reports*. Fall 2014. https://niemanreports.org/articles/who-owns-the-news-in-indonesia/

Diamond, L. (2015). Facing Up to the Democratic Recession. *Journal of Democracy*, 26(1), 141–155. doi:https://doi.org/10.1353/jod.2015.0009.

Djankov, S., McLiesh, C., Nenova, T. and Shleifer, A. (2003). Who Owns the Media? *Journal of Law and Economics*, vol. XLVI (October 2003), 341–81.

Downing, J. D. H. (2011). Media ownership, concentration, and control: the evolution of debate. In Wasko, J., Murdock, G. and Sousa, H. (eds.). *The Handbook of Political Economy of Communications*. UK: Blackwell Publishing Ltd.

Duong, M. (2017). Blogging Three Ways in Vietnam's Political Blogosphere. *Contemporary Southeast Asia: A Journal of International and Strategic Affairs* 39(2), 373–92.

Ellis, G. (2014). Keeping it in the family. In *Trust Ownership and the Future of News*. London: Palgrave Macmillan UK, pp. 99–136.

Flew, T. (2016). National media regulation in an age of convergent media: beyond globalisation, neo-liberalism and internet freedom theories. In Flew, T. et al. (eds.). *Global Media and National Policies: the Return of the State*. UK: Palgrave Macmillan.

Foa, R. S. and Mounk, Y. (2017). The Signs of Deconsolidation. *Journal of Democracy*, 28(1), 5–16.

Ford, M., Gillan, M. and Thein, H. (2016). From Cronyism to Oligarchy? Privatisation and Business Elites in Myanmar. *Journal of Contemporary Asia*, 46(1), 18–41.

Freedom House. (2017). *Freedom of the Press 2017*. Washington, DC: Freedom House. https://freedomhouse.org/report/freedom-press/freedom-press–2017

Freedom House. (2018a). *Freedom on the Net 2018: Myanmar*. Washington, DC: Freedom House. https://freedomhouse.org/report/freedom-net/2018/myanmar

Freedom House. (2018b). *Freedom on the Net 2018: the Rise of Digital Authoritarianism*. Washington, DC: Freedom House. https://freedomhouse .org/report/freedom-net/freedom-net-2018/rise-digital-authoritarianism

Garton Ash, T. (2016). *Free Speech: Ten Principles for a Connected World.* New Haven, CT: Yale University Press.

George, C. (2019). Asian Journalism. In Vos, T. P. and Hanusch, F. (eds.). *The International Encyclopedia of Journalism Studies.* New York, NY: Wiley-Blackwell.

George, C. (2017). *Singapore, Incomplete: Reflections on a First World Nation's Arrested Political Development.* Singapore: Woodsville News.

George, C. (2016). *Hate Spin: the Manufacture of Religious Offense and Its Threat to Democracy.* Cambridge, MA: The Massachusetts Institute of Technology Press.

George, C. (2007). Consolidating Authoritarian Rule: Calibrated Coercion in Singapore. *The Pacific Review* 20(2), 127–45.

George, C. (2006). *Contentious Journalism and the Internet: towards Democratic Discourse in Malaysia and Singapore.* Singapore and Seattle, WA: National University of Singapore Press and University of Washington Press.

Gomez, E.T. (2018). *Minister of Finance Incorporated: Ownership and Control of Corporate Malaysia. Institute for Democracy and Economic Affairs (IDEAS).* Palgrave Macmillan & Strategic Information and Research Development Centre.

Gong, R. (2011). Internet Politics and State Media Control: Candidate Weblogs in Malaysia. *Sociological Perspectives* 54(3), 307–28.

Hadiz, V. (2013). The Rise of Capital and the Necessity of Political Economy. *Journal of Contemporary Asia*, 43(2), 208–25.

Hadiz, V. and Robison, R. (2005). Neo-liberal Reforms and Illiberal Consolidations: the Indonesian Paradox. *The Journal of Development Studies*, 41(2), 220–41.

Hamid, S. (2018). Normalising Intolerance: Elections, Religion and Everyday Life in Indonesia. Centre for Indonesian Law, Islam and Society Policy Paper, University of Melbourne Law School.

Hanitzsch, T. (2011). Populist Disseminators, Detached Watchdogs, Critical Change Agents and Opportunist Facilitators: Professional Milieus, the Journalistic Field and Autonomy in 18 Countries. *The International Communication Gazette* 73(6), 477–94. doi: https://doi.org/https://doi.org/10.1177/1748048511412279.

Hansson, E. and Weiss, M. L. (2018). Conceptualizing political space and mobilization. In Hansson, E. and Weiss, M. L. (eds.). *Political Participation in Asia: Defining and Deploying Political Space.* London: Routledge, pp. 3–20.

Hew, W. W. (2018). Piety, Politics, and the Popularity of Felix Siauw. *New Mandala.* www.newmandala.org/piety-politics-popularity-felix-siauw/.

Houghton, T. J. and Nain, Z. (2015). 'Watchdogs or lapdogs? Monitoring Malaysia's media coverage of GE13'. In Saravanamuthu, J., Guan, L. H.

and, M. N. Mohamed Osman (eds.). *Coalitions in Collision: Malaysia's 13th General Elections.Petaling Jaya/Singapore*: SIRD/ISEAS.

Hume, E. (2004). *The Media Missionaries: American Support for Journalism Excellence and Press Freedom around the Globe.* Miami, FL: John S. and James L. Knight Foundation.

International Crisis Group (2017). *Buddhism and State Power in Myanmar.* Brussels, Belgium: International Crisis Group.

Jakarta Post. (2011, August 25). Indonesian Journalists Support Islamic Fundamentalism: Survey. Retrieved from www.thejakartapost.com/news/2011/08/25/indonesian-journalists-support-islamic-fundamentalism-survey.html

Jansen, S. C. and Martin, B. (2003). Making Censorship Backfire. *Counterpoise* 7(3), 5–15.

Jomo, K. S. (2016). The Neoliberal Counter-revolution in Retreat? *Third World Resurgence* (310/311), 6–7.

Juniarto, D. (2018). The Muslim Cyber Army: What Is It and What Does It Want? *Indonesia at Melbourne.* http://indonesiaatmelbourne.unimelb.edu.au/the-muslim-cyber-army-what-is-it-and-what-does-it-want/.

Kaufmann, D. and Bellver, A. (2005). Transparenting Transparency: Initial Empirics and Policy Applications. *SSRN.* http://dx.doi.org/10.2139/ssrn.808664

Kemp, S. (2018). The State of the Internet in Q4 2018. We Are Social. *The Next Web* (17 October) https://thenextweb.com/contributors/2018/10/17/q4-2018-internet-report-almost-4–2-billion-humans-are-online/

Klimkiewicz, B. (2009). Structural Media Pluralism and Ownership Revisited: the Case of Central and Eastern Europe. *Journal of Media Business Studies*, 6(3), 43–62.

Kunkler, M. (2013). How pluralist democracy became the consensual discourse among secular and nonsecular Muslims in Indonesia. In Kunkler, M. and Stepan, A. (eds.). *Democracy and Islam in Indonesia.* New York: Columbia University Press, pp. 53–72.

Lakhdhir, L. (2015). *Creating a Culture of Fear: The Criminalization of Peaceful Expression in Malaysia.* New York, NY: Human Rights Watch.

Lall, M. (2016). *Understanding Reform in Myanmar: People and Society in the Wake of Military Rule.* London: Hurst Publishers.

Lewis, G. (2006). *Virtual Thailand: The Media and Cultural Politics in Thailand, Malaysia and Singapore.* Routledge.

Lim, M. (2012). *The League of Thirteen: Media Concentration in Indonesia. Research Report.* Tempe, AZ: Participatory Media Law at Arizona State University. www.public.asu.edu/~mlim4/files/Lim_IndoMediaOwnership_2012.pdf.

Lowry, C., and Littlejohn, S. (2006). Dialogue and the Discourse of Peacebuilding in Maluku, Indonesia. *Conflict Resolution Quarterly* 23(4), 409–26.

Mansor, L. (2017, May 8). Media Prima Buys Rev Asia Unit in Landmark Deal. *New Straits Times*. www.nst.com.my/business/2017/05/237436/media-prima-buys-rev-asia-unit-landmark-deal (accessed 2 October 2018)

Marston, J. (1996). Cambodian news media in the UNTAC period and after. In Heder, S. and Ledgerwood, J. (Eds.). *Propaganda, Politics and Violence in Cambodia: Democratic transition under United Nations peace-keeping* (pp. 208–43). Armonk, NY: M. E. Sharpe.

Masduki. (2017). Media and Politics: Re-Thinking the Indonesian Broadcasting System. *Jurnal Ilmu Sosial dan Ilmu Politik*, 21(1), 14–27.

Maza, C. (2018, July 28). Cambodia Elections 2018: Democracy Died Long before People Cast Their Votes, Experts Say. *Newsweek*. www.newsweek.com/cambodia-elections-democracy-died-people-polls-1040387

McCargo, D. (2017). Mediatized Populisms: New Media, New Partisanship: Divided Virtual Politics In and Beyond Thailand. *International Journal of Communication* 11, 4138–57.

McCargo, D. (2003). *Media and Politics in Pacific Asia*. RoutledgeCurzon.

McChesney, R. (1998). Making Media Democratic. *Boston Review* (Summer). https://bostonreview.net/archives/BR23.3/mcchesney.html.

Media Development Investment Fund. (2018). *An Unfavorable Business: Running Local Media in Myanmar's Ethnic States and Regions*. NY: Media Development Investment Fund. www.mdif.org/wp-content/uploads/2018/11/An-Unfavorable-Business-MDIF-report.pdf.

Mellado, C., Hellmueller, L., Márquez-Ramírez, M., Humanes, M. L., Sparks, C., Stepinska, A., . . . Wang, H. (2017). The Hybridization of Journalistic Cultures: a Comparative Study of Journalistic Role Performance. *Journal of Communication* 67(6), 944–967. doi:https://doi.org/10.1111/jcom.12339.

Milton, A. K. (2001). Bound but not Gagged: Media Reform in Democratic Transitions. *Comparative Political Studies* 34(5), 493–526. https://doi.org/10.1177/0010414001034005002.

Mishra, P. (2017). *Age of Anger*. New York, NY: Farrar, Straus and Giroux.

Morozov, E. (2012). *The Net Delusion: The Dark Side of Internet Freedom*. New York, NY: Public Affairs.

Myers, M. and Angaya Juma L. (2018) *Defending Independent Media: A Comprehensive Analysis of Aid Flows*. Washington DC: Center for International Media Assistance (CIMA). www.cima.ned.org/publication/cmprehensive-analysis-media-aid-flows/.

Nain, Z. and Venkiteswaran, G. (2016). Local Media and Digital Frontiers: The Malaysian Conundrum. *Media Development*, 3/2016. World Association for Christian Communication.

Nain, Z. and Wang, L. K. (2004). Ownership, control and the Malaysian media. In Thomas, P. N. and Nain, Z. (Eds.). *Who Owns the Media?: Global Trends and Local Resistances. (249–270)*. Southbound, Zed Books and World Association for Christian Communication.

Noam, E.M (2016). *Who Owns the World's Media? Media Concentration and Ownership around the World*. Oxford University Press.

Norris, P. and Odugbemi, S. (2010). Evaluating media performance. In Norris, P. (ed.). *Public Sentinel: News Media & Governance Reform*. Washington, DC: World Bank Publications, pp. 3–29.

Nugroho, Y., Putri, D. and Laksmi, S. (2012). Mapping the Landscape of the Media Industry in Contemporary Indonesia. *Research Report*. Jakarta: Center for Innovation Policy and Governance and HIVOS Regional Office Southeast Asia.

O'Connor, T. (2017). Intolerance in the Mainstream. *Peace Review* 29(2), 184–91. doi:https://doi.org/10.1080/10402659.2017.1308724.

Oster, J. (2015). *Media Freedom as a Fundamental Right*. Cambridge University Press.

Pascual, J. (2017). Press under Siege: Media Organizations as Targets of the State. *Media Times*. Manila: Centre for Media Freedom and Responsibility. http://mediatimes.cmfr-phil.org/press-under-siege-media-organizations-as-targets-of-the-state/ (accessed 29 September 2018).

Peruško, Z. (2013). What Went Wrong With Media Reforms in Post-Socialist Europe. *Media Watch*. Retrieved from bib.irb.hr/prikazi-rad?rad=658264

Pornwasin, A. (2017, June 26). Controversy over Regulation of OTT Content on Internet. *The Nation*. www.nationmultimedia.com/news/national/30319085 (accessed 2 October 2018).

Price, M. and Krug, P. (2000). *The Enabling Environment for Free and Independent Media*. Programme in Comparative Media Law & Policy, Oxford University.

Price, M., Rozumilowicz, B. & Verhulst S. (Eds.). (2002). *Media Reform: Democratizing the Media, Democratizing the State*. Routledge.

Puddington, A. (2017). *Breaking Down Democracy: Goals, Strategies, and Methods of Modern Authoritarians*. Washington, DC: Freedom House.

Rodan, G. (2004). *Transparency and Authoritarian Rule in Southeast Asia: Singapore and Malaysia*. London; New York: RoutledgeCurzon.

Romano, A. (2009). Asia. In Norris, P. (ed.). *Public Sentinel: News Media & Governance Reform*. Washington, DC: World Bank Publications, pp. 353–75.

Rothman, P. (2015). *The Politics of Media Development: The Importance of Engaging Government and Civil Society*. Center for International Media Assistance, National Endowment for Democracy.

Schiffrin, A. (2017). *In the Service of Power: Media Capture and the Threat to Democracy*. National Endowment for Democracy and the Center for International Media Assistance.

Schlosberg, J. (2017). *Media Ownership and Agenda Control: The hidden limits of the information age*. New York & London: Routledge.

Schudson, M. (2011). *The Sociology of News*. W. W. Norton & Company, Inc.

Segura, M. & S. Waisbord. (2016). *Media Movements: Civil Society and Media Policy Reform in Latin America*. London: Zed Books.

Sen, K. and Hill, D. (2011) (Eds.), *Politics and the Media in Twenty-First Century Indonesia: Decade of Democracy*. New York & London: Routledge.

Shin, D.C. (2015). Cultural Hybridization in East Asia: Exploring an Alternative to the Global Democratization Thesis. *Journal of Elections, Public Opinion and Parties* 25(1), 10–30. doi:https://doi.org/10.1080/17457289.2014.953009.

Siriyuvasak, U. (2001). Regulation, Reform and the Question of Democratizing the Broadcast Media in Thailand. *Javnost-the Public*, 8(2), 89–107.

Splichal, S. (2004). Privatization: The cost of media democratization in East and Central Europe? In Thomas, P. N. and Nain, Z. (Eds.). *Who Owns the Media?: Global Trends and Local Resistances* (pp. 51–68). Southbound, Zed Books and World Association for Christian Communication.

Steele, J. (2018). *Mediating Islam: Cosmopolitan Journalisms in Muslim Southeast Asia*. Seattle: University of Washington Press.

Steele, J. (2012). The Making of the 1999 Indonesian Press Law. *Indonesia*, 94, 1–22.

Steele, J. (2005). *Wars Within: The Story of Tempo, an Independent Magazine in Soeharto's Indonesia*. Jakarta & Singapore: PT Equinox Publishing Indonesia and Institute of Southeast Asian Studies.

Sudibyo, A. and Patria, N. (2013). The Television Industry in Post-authoritarian Indonesia. *Journal of Contemporary Asia*, 43(2), 257–75.

Tai, Q. (2014). China's Media Censorship: a Dynamic and Diversified Regime. *Journal of East Asian Studies* 14(2), 185–209.

Tapsell, R. (2018). New media, old rule in Malaysia. In Lopez, G. and Welsh, B. (eds.). *Regime Resilience in Malaysia and Singapore*. Petaling Jaya,

Malaysia: Strategic Information and Research Development Centre, pp. 129–43.

Tapsell, R. (2017). The political economy of digital media. In Jurriens, E. and Tapsell, R. (Eds.). *Digital Indonesia: Connectivity and Divergence*, pp. 56–74. Singapore: ISEAS-Yusof Ishak Institute.

Tapsell, R. (2015). *Indonesia's Media Oligarchy and the 'Jokowi Phenomenon'* in Indonesia, 99, 29–50.

Tapsell, R. (2013). Negotiating Media 'Balance' in Malaysia's 2013 General Election. *Journal of Current Southeast Asian Affairs* 32(2), 39–60.

Tapsell, R. (2010). Stopping the Flow. *Inside Indonesia* (Jul–Sep 2010). www .insideindonesia.org/stopping-the-flow.

The Edge Financial Daily. (2017, August 16). Astro May Face Pressure from Ansa. www.theedgemarkets.com/article/astro-may-face-pressure-ansa.

Thomas, P. N. and Nain, Z. (Eds.) (2014). *Who Owns the Media?: Global Trends and Local Resistances*. Southbound, Zed Books and World Association for Christian Communication.

Transparency International (2017). *Corruption Perceptions Index 2016*. Berlin, Germany: Transparency International.

Triyono, H. (2018). Don Bosco: Perintah Bang Surya, you bantu Jokowi. *Beritagar* (26 November 2018). https://beritagar.id/artikel/bincang/don-bosco-perintah-bang-surya-you-bantu-jokowi (accessed 2 May 2019).

Tunsarawuth, S. (2018). *Thailand – 'Reform' Further Restricts Free Speech and Media.* Annual Report. Southeast Asian Press Alliance. www.seapa.org/thailand-reform-further-restricts-free-speech-and-media/ (accessed 26 September 2018).

Turner, G. (2016). The nation-state and media globalisation: has the nation-state returned – or did it never leave? In Flew, T. et al. (Eds.). *Global Media and National Policies: The Return of the State (Chapter 6)*. UK: Palgrave Macmillan.

UNDP (2018). *Human Development Indices and Indicators: 2018 Statistical Update.* New York, NY: United Nations Development Programme. www .hdr.undp.org/en/content/human-development-indices-indicators-2018-statisti cal-update.

UNESCO (2018a).*World Trends in Freedom of Expression and Media Development: 2017/2018 Global Report. Paris*, France: UN Educational, Scientific and Cultural Organization. https://en.unesco.org/world-media-trends-2017.

UNESCO (2018b). *UNESCO Observatory of Killed Journalists.* https://en .unesco.org/themes/safety-journalists/observatory.

UNESCO (2008). *Media Development Indicators: A Framework for Assessing Media Development.* https://unesdoc.unesco.org/ark:/48223/pf0000163102

UN Human Rights Council (2012). *Report of the Special Rapporteur on the Promotion and Protection of the Right to Freedom of Opinion and Expression, Frank La Rue.* A/HRC/20/17. www.refworld.org/docid/5008134b2.html.

Van Bruinessen, M. (2011). *What Happened to the Smiling Face of Indonesian Islam? Muslim Intellectualism and the Conservative Turn in Post-Suharto Indonesia.* Singapore: S. Rajaratnam School of International Studies.

Venkiteswaran, G., Yin Yadanar Thein and Myint Kyaw. (2019). Legal changes for media and expression: New reforms, old controls. In Brooten, L., McElhone, J. M. and Venkiteswaran, G. (eds.). *Myanmar Media in Transition: Legacies, Challenges and Change.* Singapore: ISEAS Publishing, pp. 59–94.

Voltmer, K. (2013). *The Media in Transitional Democracies.* Polity Press.

Weiss, M. (2014). New Media, New Activism: Trends and Trajectories in Malaysia, Singapore and Indonesia. *International Development Planning Review* 36(1), 91–109. https://doi.org/10.3828/idpr.2014.6.

Weiss, M. L. and Hansson, E. (2017). Participation and space: Themes, patterns, and implications. In Hansson, E. and Weiss, M. L. (eds.). *Political Participation in Asia: Defining and Deploying Political Space.* Abingdon, Oxford: Routledge, pp. 206–11.

Whitehead, L. (2002). *Democratization: Theory and Experience.* Oxford University Press.

Wijayanto. (2017). Fearing the Majority: Catholic Media in Muslim Indonesia. *Media Asia* 44(1), 33–39. https://doi.org/10.1080/01296612.2017.1374319.

Zittrain, J. (2008). *The Future of the Internet – and How to Stop It.* New Haven and London: Yale University Press.

Acknowledgements

The authors wish to thank their respective institutions, Hong Kong Baptist University's School of Communication and the University of Nottingham Malaysia's School of Media, Languages and Cultures, for providing an environment conducive to international research. Part of the research for this Element was supported by the SHAPE-SEA Programme funded by SIDA.

Dedicated to all Southeast Asians struggling for freedom of expression

Cambridge Elements ≡

Politics and Society in Southeast Asia

Edward Aspinall
Australian National University
Edward Aspinall is a professor of politics at the Coral Bell School of Asia-Pacific Affairs, Australian National University. A specialist of Southeast Asia, especially Indonesia, much of his research has focused on democratisation, ethnic politics and civil society in Indonesia and, most recently, clientelism across Southeast Asia.

Meredith L. Weiss
University at Albany, SUNY
Meredith L. Weiss is Professor of Political Science at the University at Albany, SUNY. Her research addresses political mobilization and contention, the politics of identity and development, and electoral politics in Southeast Asia, with particular focus on Malaysia and Singapore.

About the Series
The Elements series Politics and Society in Southeast Asia includes both country-specific and thematic studies on one of the world's most dynamic regions. Each title, written by a leading scholar of that country or theme, combines a succinct, comprehensive, up-to-date overview of debates in the scholarly literature with original analysis and a clear argument.

Cambridge Elements ☰

Politics and Society in Southeast Asia

Elements in the Series

Indonesia: Twenty Years after Democracy
Jamie Davidson

Civil–Military Relations in Southeast Asia
Aurel Croissant

Singapore: Identity, Brand, Power
Kenneth Paul Tan

Ritual and Region: The Invention of ASEAN
Mathew Davies

Populism in Southeast Asia
Paul Kenny

Cambodia: Return to Authoritarianism
Kheang Un

Vietnam: A Pathway from State Socialism
Thaveeporn Vasavakul

Independent Timor-Leste: Regime, Economy and Identity
Douglas Kammen

Media and Power in Southeast Asia
Cherian George and Gayathry Venkiteswaran

A full series listing is available at: www.cambridge.org/ESEA

Printed in the United States
By Bookmasters